NO PLACE FOR GOD

MOYRA DOORLY

NO PLACE FOR GOD

*The Denial of the Transcendent
in Modern Church Architecture*

IGNATIUS PRESS　SAN FRANCISCO

Photograph by Gerald A. Naus

Cover design by John Herreid

© 2007 Ignatius Press, San Francisco
ISBN 978-1-58617-153-7
Library of Congress Control Number 2006921209
Printed in the United States of America ∞

CONTENTS

PREFACE

The first time I set foot inside a modern Catholic church was in 1994. The interior resembled a conference hall or seminar room with plain and functional furniture, a sound system, carpets everywhere, and meaningless splash paintings on the walls. The exterior could have belonged to any other modern building in the town, a health center perhaps, or a public library.

That was the year I converted to Catholicism. More used to the beautiful Catholic churches of southern Europe and the simple but charming chapel in the remote parish where I lived, this new building came as a shock. Later I was told it had won two architectural awards, and I wondered how this could be. The reply was that the church had been designed to involve the community and encourage everyone in the town to see the building as theirs, not just to be another over-decorated edifice triumphantly proclaiming its message to the world.

Having studied architecture in the late 1970s, I was familiar with the Modernist style and its critics. A consensus had emerged during this period that the massive urban redevelopments of previous decades had been a disaster and Modernist ideas about space were among the prime causes.

It seemed to me that although these ideas had been denounced twenty years previously, they were still influencing the design of award-winning, new style churches. Perhaps this was because Modernism's earlier critics had been chiefly concerned with its impact on the secular urban environment.

No Place for God: The Denial of the Transcendent in Contemporary Church Architecture is an attempt, therefore, to examine Modernism's impact on church design and ask whether Modernist ideas about space are having as adverse an effect on the church building as they did on the secular.

A Great Building Disaster

The modern age has witnessed the construction of the most banal and uninspiring churches in history. The attempt to create a church architecture that would meet the needs of the age has resulted in churches that are unfit for any age. Contemporary church buildings, as well as being the ugliest ever built, are also the emptiest.

Many atheists used to say that whatever they felt about religion, it was impossible not to admire church architecture. But now there is hardly a Catholic who can admire (modern) church architecture. Today's churches no longer point to a transcendent God, a God who inspires awe, reverence, and wonder. Today's churches are geared almost entirely to the celebration of the people who happen to be present because that is where God now is, within the worshipping community.

According to G. K. Chesterton, "Of all horrible religions the most horrible is the worship of the God within. . . . That Jones shall worship the God within him turns out ultimately to mean that Jones shall worship Jones." [1] Men have always attempted to make magnificent and beautiful the buildings dedicated to the gods that are without. But when the god is within, what happens to the building? A glance at what passes for a church today reveals the answer, but the appearance is only a symptom. The underlying problem

---

[1] G. K. Chesterton, *Orthodoxy* (San Francisco: Ignatius Press, 1995), 81.

is that the contemporary church building is hardly a church at all. Instead it is more a temple to the spirit of the age.

When the liturgical revolution of the twentieth century deliberately shifted the focus of the Church's worship to God present in the people, this went hand in hand with a profound change in the idea of what a church is, how it functions, and the message it should proclaim. The modernizers claim, with justification, that church architecture has always responded to the needs of the times. Over the centuries, the Church has adopted the stylistic and aesthetic ideas of the ages and fashioned her church buildings accordingly, thereby creating an architectural heritage that includes the wonders of the Romanesque, the Gothic, the Renaissance, and the Baroque. Accordingly, the claim is that the changes being undertaken today are simply the latest in a series of adaptations the Church has made to her buildings and liturgy. Future generations will look back on the churches of today with the same admiration we hold for the great churches of the past.

In fact what has been done to the church building in recent decades, and is still being done, is unprecedented in the history of the Church. So radical is the break from tradition that the term "revolution" is barely adequate to describe what has happened. The later half of the twentieth century saw a lot of church buildings commissioned, designed, and constructed, the majority of them in the Modernist style, with its pared-down and stripped minimalism, its horror of ornament, and its rejection of narrative imagery in favor of the abstract. This was the predominant style of the twentieth century, and it could therefore be argued that today's baleful church buildings are simply the result of the Church having done what she has done for centuries, which is to embrace the architectural aesthetic of the age.

Consequently, the merits, or lack of merits, of the Modernist style are merely a question of taste.

However, architecture is about more than appearances, and this is as true for the Modernist style as it is for any other. Of chief importance to the characteristics of any style of architecture are the spatial principles that determine them. The reason for this is that buildings, by their very nature, enclose space. There is no way around it. As soon as four walls are built and covered with a roof, space is enclosed. This is how buildings perform their function, which is basically to provide shelter and contain the activities carried on within them.

But the spaces that buildings create also carry meaning that goes beyond their functional use. Because the art of architecture is concerned with the creation and manipulation of space, the aesthetic of a particular style necessarily grows out of the same principles governing the use of space by that style. The appearance of buildings is therefore determined as much by the ideas about space that predominate in a particular age as it is by the tastes and preferences of that age.

Therefore it is the adoption of Modernist *spatial* principles, as well as Modernist aesthetics, that sets the recent changes to the church building so apart from the historical developments preceding them. It would have been possible for the Church to have embraced one without the other, and this is what happened in the earlier decades of the twentieth century, before the Liturgical Movement promoting the revolution really began to gain ground. The first churches to be built according to the Modernist aesthetic may have featured plain glass instead of stained glass, large areas of bare concrete, and an almost complete lack of decoration, but they didn't make a full break from the traditional church form. If this had continued, if the Church had adopted the

Modernist aesthetic and rejected Modernist ideas about space, then the solution to the current problem, the problem of ugly churches, would be simple. A restyling exercise would be required, that is all: a painting and decoration job, a make-over to render beautiful the bare concrete, the exposed steel beams, and the barren brickwork.

But the situation has gone far beyond that because the Church *did* adopt Modernist ideas about space, ideas entirely in tune with contemporary self-reverence. This happened with a vengeance during the years immediately following the Second Vatican Council, when the development of a new liturgical style created the impetus for the complete dismantling of the traditional church form. As a result, the Catholic Church, which for nearly two millennia inspired buildings of magnificence and beauty, has reached the stage of building churches that are hardly churches at all. Because Modernist architecture is the architecture of Relativist space, by adopting the Modernist style, the Church has incorporated Relativism into her very fabric. That is the argument here. But what does it mean? What is Relativist space?

Relativist space is homogenous, directionless, and value-free. In other words, it is the same everywhere you look, and no part of it has any more significance than any other part. In the Relativist universe, there are no signposts and no obvious paths forward, because no place has any more or less meaning than here. In Relativist space, boundaries and distinctions are dissolved, and since the concept of a special place set apart is an alien one, sacred space, by definition, cannot exist. Therefore in a universe from which the sacred has been eliminated, the only place for the individual to look is within.

These are the ideas about space that are embodied in the Modernist style. They also characterize the model of the universe as conceived by the modern age. Space, that is, outer space or universal space, has a form and an architecture that is reflected in the architecture of buildings. The medieval cathedrals, with their verticality, their hierarchy of spaces, and distinctions between spaces were the perfect embodiment of the medieval universe, which was also vertical, hierarchical, and marked by distinctions between Heaven and earth, between the sacred and the profane.

That the Church has embraced the concept of Relativist space is evidenced by the liturgical revolution that took place after the Second Vatican Council. When the Church adopted the new liturgy, existing churches began to be "reordered" so that they could best reflect new ideas about the celebration of the Mass, and new church buildings were designed with an internal layout that had never been seen before in the history of the Church. The casual visitor to the nearby Catholic church cannot help but be aware of the changes that were implemented, in many cases, against the wishes of the congregation.

The most obvious has been the reorientation of the priest so that Mass is said facing the people. This innovation says loud and clear that there is nothing to look to that is outside the community. It represents a denial of the transcendent in favor of the immanent. This is even more marked in churches where seating is arranged to create a circular or semicircular layout, where there is nothing beyond the priest at the altar than more people facing the altar. Circles by their very nature are inward-looking forms.

In existing churches, reordering schemes have seen elaborate high altars removed and replaced with new and much simpler table altars, which have been pushed forward into the nave so that the people can "gather round". The choir may be relocated so as to appear less distinct from the laity.

1
Parish Church of Oberkirch, Basel, Switzerland.
Interior before 1973 reordering.

2
Parish Church of Oberkirch, Basel, Switzerland.
Interior after 1973 reordering.

Statues have been removed, frescos and murals have been whitewashed over, and sanctuary rails have been discarded so as to lessen the distinction between the sanctuary and nave. Pews have been taken out and replaced with plastic stacking chairs in the name of greater flexibility.

The aim has been to create a sense of informality and encourage spontaneity of worship, to break down barriers between the clergy and the laity, and to emphasize the church as belonging to the community by accommodating social activities into the body of the building. Churches, or rather "places of worship", are intended to be welcoming so that people can feel at home and relax. To this end, no effort is spared in designing new church buildings that do not look like churches and are hard to distinguish from the local library or health center. That is the intention. A church that looks like a church might put people off.

Internally, traditional linear forms are rejected as being too hierarchical and authoritarian. Instead, the preferred arrangement is circular, modeled on the theater in the round or the seminar room. How better to demonstrate the gathering of the community? The language is itself revealing. The nave, the sanctuary, the baptistry—these are out of fashion. The preferred term is the "worship space", which can double as a meeting area or a location for social activities.

It is not going too far to say that the new liturgy has an architecture, or a form and a structure, that can be examined for what it says about ideas of space. It is not within the scope of this argument to discuss recent developments such as the introduction of the vernacular into the Mass, or the suitability of overenthusiastic gestures during the kiss of peace, or whether Holy Communion should be received standing or kneeling, in the hand or on the tongue. For the purposes of this discussion, the most relevant question is to

3
Saint Joseph's Church, Epsom, Surrey, England, 2001.
Exterior.

4
Saint Joseph's Church, Epsom, Surrey, England, 2001.
Interior.

what extent the new liturgy reflects the preference for the relativizing of space that is the mark of the modern age.

The image of the "People of God gathered around the altar", which the Modernists have advanced as the inspiration for the new church building, could only be possible in a Relativist universe in which no absolute or objective truth can be said to exist *out there* and in which all reality is subjectively determined. Modernists claim that Mass facing the people was the practice of the early Church (which it was not), and that Mass was said facing the people in the Constantinian basilicas (which was not the case either).

Another sign that the new liturgy reflects the Relativism of the age is the pattern of movements made by the various participants at the Mass. This pattern is generated by the constant coming and going and endless bustle that indicates the formlessness of Relativist space, its lack of direction, and its denial of the sacred. There is a constant movement from nave to sanctuary and back again, if indeed there is any boundary between them at all. Lay people enter the sanctuary to give the readings, and priest wanders about in the nave to deliver his sermon through a mobile microphone. Holy Communion is brought into the nave for distribution; and there is movement across the aisles during the kiss of peace. The flow of the Mass is frequently interrupted by every party having to do its bit. The whole thing seems scattered, its movements characterized by a breaking down of form.

The traditional linear arrangements had a structure and direction that could be readily understood and in which it was possible to be at rest. In a Relativist universe emptied of meaning, it is a very human response to fill the vacated spaces with noise and activity. Is it any wonder that the New Mass is the way it is?

There has been much discussion recently about how authentic the implementation of the Second Vatican Council has been. Did the Council intend the huge changes that have taken place, or have its documents been liberally interpreted and the results attributed to some indefinable and nebulous "spirit of Vatican II"? A detailed discussion of this is also beyond the scope of the argument here, but the design of the contemporary church building displays the influence of the spirit of Relativism at every turn. The styles of the past embodied ideas about space and Man's relation to God that were in harmony with the traditional teachings of the Church. It is possible to hold a personal preference for one or the other of these styles, because the theology they expressed remained more or less consistent. The Modernist church style, however, is theologically unsound.

Modernist architecture has been as harmful to the Church as it was to our towns and cities. We still have to live with much of the havoc caused by the massive urban developments of postwar decades, but thankfully many secular builders have abandoned the destructive ideas about space promoted by the Modernists. State governments and the architectural firms they employ also have moved on from Modernism.

Unfortunately the same cannot be said for many of our church designers. Recent decades have seen fads in church design come and go, like the concrete Brutalism of the 1950s and '60s and the understated, civic look that was designed to disappear into the municipal background. Then came the homely, community aesthetic intended to be as unchallenging as possible and, most recently, the dazzlingly lit, white box which resembles the style of the latest art gallery or sushi bar. But no matter how the fashions have changed, the same Relativist ideas about space have remained. It is

5
Saint John's Abbey, Collegeville, Minnesota, U.S.A., 1961.
Architect—Marcel Breuer.
Exterior.

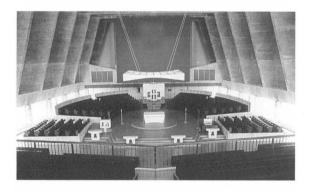

6
Saint John's Abbey, Collegeville, Minnesota, U.S.A., 1961.
Architect—Marcel Breuer.
Interior.

often said that churches represent "theology in stone" and
that they can be "read" as such. If this is true for the Gothic
cathedral, with its towering internal spaces pointing to God
and its abundance of imagery offering instruction and inspiration to the laity, then it is equally true for the emptied
church buildings of today. Emptiness can speak volumes,
just as silence can be deafening.

If buildings speak to us, what does this new church architecture say about the state of Christianity today? It has been
said that the motto of the modern age is "No particular

7
Parish Church, Riola di Vergato, near Bologna, Italy, 1978.
Architect—Alvar Aalto.
Exterior.

8
Parish Church, Riola di Vergato, near Bologna, Italy, 1978.
Architect—Alvar Aalto.
Interior.

place to go". In a Relativist age, the sign over the church door might as well be "Nothing special here". The new ideas about style and worship represent a profound shift away from the concept of the church building as a "House of

God" toward the concept of a church as a place where the "People of God" gather.

Throughout the centuries, whatever the aesthetics and form of a particular style, whether a plain and simple chapel or grand and ornate cathedral, the church building was able to embody a vision that was both immanent *and* transcendent. In other words, "God is with us" and at the same time God is entirely "Other". But Relativism denies the transcendent vision and is all on the side of subjectivity.

By embracing the spirit of the age, the Church has necessarily become watered-down and bland, fearful of proclaiming the glory of God and anxious to please. By attempting to become more "relevant" to the age, she has only succeeded in becoming more and more marginalized. The church building, once the House of God and a foretaste of Heaven, is no place in particular and nothing special. The overwhelming impression given by the ever-decreasing numbers of people still worshipping there is of inward-looking and self-celebratory communities who barely know or acknowledge, let alone rejoice in, the presence of God or the great wonders of the faith.

Many commentators have noted with regret the elimination of mystery, awe, and reverence from the contemporary Church and her liturgy. Just as regrettable, surely, is the impulse toward self-worship that has declared the contemporary church building to be "no place for God".

The Spirit of the Age

By definition, the spirit of the age, any age, is something transitory, something that will pass away as time moves on.

But while it is here and exerting its influence, is the spirit of an age merely a complex of ideas, or something unifying that complex of ideas, something that cannot itself be broken down into constituent parts?

The aim of this chapter is to examine several ideas proposed in the modern age and look for signs of a common spirit animating and uniting them. At first glance, these ideas could appear to be independent of each other. For instance, what does Theosophy have in common with neopaganism, and what can evolution possibly have in common with either? The point of the argument here is to find a single idea or train of thought running through them.

On the face of it, only Einstein's theories of relativity would seem to have a direct connection to the spirit of Relativism that permeates the modern age and informs its outlook, while psychoanalysis might appear to have none at all. But if they are examined for the following characteristics, similarities emerge. These characteristics are:

— the denial of absolutes,

— the elevation of the subjective over the objective,

— the pursuit of constant change because of the belief that change, of itself, is progress.

A man possessed by the spirit of Relativism cannot accept as valid any opinion or version of reality originating from outside himself. He might accept as "truths" those "facts" that can be scientifically measured and demonstrated, but even those might prove to be temporary. Meanwhile, every proposition or opinion that lies beyond the scope of modern science is merely relative to the subjective experiences or "beliefs" of individuals. The Relativist is unable to examine philosophically whether a particular opinion, either belonging to himself or someone else, is true or not. As a result, no "inner truth" discovered even by the Relativist himself can be known by him as actually true, otherwise it would resemble an absolute, which cannot exist.

The Relativist has no one but himself and nothing but his own subjective experience to depend upon. He cannot base his actions, tastes or preferences on any principles or convictions, and he will be subject to his changing whims or his society's changing fashions. The Relativist spirit, therefore, is a restless spirit, seeking constant change in a universe where nothing is fixed.

1. Einstein's Theories of Relativity

It has been said that the modern age began in 1915 with the publication of Einstein's general theory of relativity. His theories were an answer to the already well-known and subsequently repeated Michelson-Morley experiment of 1887, which showed that light does not obey the laws of Newtonian physics.[1]

---

[1] Margaret Wertheim, *The Pearly Gates of Cyberspace: A History of Space from Dante to the Internet* (London: Virago Press, 1999), 185.

For example, if two cars traveling toward one another, each at 40 miles per hour, collide head on, their impact speed will be 40 plus 40 miles per hour, that is, 80 miles per hour. This explains why head-on collisions are so often fatal. Now apparently light travels at a speed of 186,000 miles per second. According to Newton, if you were to travel toward a light source at a speed of, say, 1,000 miles per second, the velocity of the light relative to you would be 186,000 plus 1,000 miles per second, that is, 187,000 miles per second.

But the Michelson-Morley experiment repeatedly showed that regardless of the speed of the observer, light always appeared to travel at 186,000 miles per second. The question provoked by the experiment was, if I am traveling at a different speed than you, how can light appear to travel at the same speed relative to both of us? Einstein dispensed with the idea that individuals shared a single universal space in which Newton's absolute laws operated. Instead he claimed that each individual occupies his own space in which the speed of light is always constant for that person.

This was the final step in the dismantling of the previous model that had endured from the time of Aristotle, until Galileo's observations began the process of tearing it down. One of its significant features had been the distinction between the earth and the heavens, between the terrestrial and the celestial realms. The celestial realm lay beyond the orbit of the moon and was eternal and immutable, while below the moon everything was temporal and changeable.

When Galileo saw spots on the sun and craters on the moon through his telescope, the boundary between the two realms was dissolved. What had once been the everlasting celestial realm suddenly appeared subject to change and decay. Then according to Newton, who was born in the year Galileo died, the same laws of gravity and motion that operated on earth operated throughout the universe. The celestial realm had been rubbed out of the picture.

But the Newtonian model still admitted the existence of absolutes. The same law of gravity causing the apple to fall from the tree and the planets to maintain their orbits, had been formulated and put into action by a divine Creator. In a universe governed by absolute laws, there was still room for the Creator who made them, even if there was no pin-pointed place in the heavens where He dwelled with the angels and saints.

With Einstein's theory of relativity, the desacralization of the universe begun by Galileo was complete, and the social impact of this was staggering. During the 1920s, people began to assume that if the universe lacked absolute laws of motion, then perhaps it lacked absolute moral laws as well. "Mistakenly but perhaps inevitably, relativity became confused with [moral] relativism." [2] It was supposed that in a Relativist universe everything depends upon the point of view of the observer, not just the speed of light. What may be "true" for an individual in certain circumstances may not be "true" for an individual in different circumstances. "Everything is relative" is the mantra of the age. No longer was any objective truth held to exist "out there", and with that went faith in a transcendent God.

In the Relativist universe, man can travel for an eternity through unbounded and infinite space and still be nowhere of any greater significance than where he started from. All possibilities and unlimited freedoms exist out there, but which way should a man go when there is nothing but empty and meaningless space?

---

[2] Paul Johnson, *Modern Times: The World from the Twenties to the Eighties* (New York: Harper and Row Publishers, Inc., 1983), 4.

In the face of so much nothingness, there is only one direction to look, and that is inward. In a universe emptied of the divine and in which absolutes cannot exist, the only truth with any meaning is to be found within the individual. And since truth is subjectively determined, there can be no single body of truth, only a multiplicity of equally valid truths. Consequently, whatever is right for one may not be right for another, and vice versa. In such a universe, the only really acceptable god is "the god of my own understanding", a view neatly summed up in the expression "May your god go with you."

2. Theosophy

Helena Petrovna Blavatsky co-founded the Theosophical Society in 1875, and her ideas are said to have been admired by Hitler. Apparently she was given her insights by one or more of the spirits of ascended Tibetan masters while traveling in the Himalayas. These "immortals" she termed the "Masters of the Hidden Brotherhood" or "Mahatmas", and she claimed to be in regular contact with them throughout her life.

Also known as Madam Blavatsky, she is sometimes described as the godmother of the New Age movement, and her embracing of Eastern spiritual traditions is certainly one of that movement's hallmarks, as is her emphasis on the individual search for inner truth. Theosophy encouraged the study of comparative religion and challenged the notion that any one religion has greater access to the truth than any other. The ideas proposed by this little-known society have had an incalculable impact upon the consciousness of the modern age.

In theosophy all the world religions are presented as equally valid because they are each manifestations of the same great universal spirit underlying and uniting everything that exists. The world religions, according to the Theosophists, have become paralyzed by tradition and smothered by the unnecessary accumulations of the centuries. Therefore in order to reach the one essential truth or great reality that is beyond all the gods, the dogmas and creeds that divide and hinder must be discarded.

Christ, the Buddha, Vishnu, Mohammed, these are wise teachers sent by the great universal spirit, but none of them has an exclusive claim to the truth. It is therefore up to the discerning individual to search for the reality behind the religions of the world and not to be constricted by any one tradition. There can be no right or wrong way of doing things, only different and equally valid ways. Tradition and authority mean oppression. The only certainty is human intuition. The only true guide is the self.

Underlying Theosophy is the idea of the essential oneness of all beings. Life throughout the cosmos originates from the same divine source or consciousness, and everything that exists contains this consciousness within it. Some may choose to call this consciousness God. Theosophists call it Logos, and since Logos resides in everyone, it is the task of the individual to perfect the Logos within. Many people are unaware of their own divine nature, until they awaken to it. The word *theosophy* derives from the Greek *theos* (god, divinity) and *sophia* (wisdom).

A single lifetime may not be long enough for the individual to realize his divine nature, and so reincarnation is an important component of Theosophy. So is evolution, which is claimed to be part of the divine plan. All forms of life are continually evolving and reincarnating until they reach the state of wisdom necessary to ascend to divinity. The aims of the Theosophical Society can be summed up as—the formation of a universal brotherhood of mankind without distinction of race, creed, sex, caste, or color; the study of comparative religion, philosophy, and science; and the investigation of both the unexplained laws of nature and the powers latent in Man.[3]

The claim that there had once existed a single spiritual system of which the world religions contain only a trace, thereby denying the specific claims of Christianity, was made increasingly during the nineteenth century. Although Madam Blavatsky's particular interest was in the religious traditions of the East, there were other figures of the time who sought to elevate the status of the ancient religions of the West by claiming that the Druids, the ancient Celts, the Egyptians, et cetera, had a truer knowledge of the great universal spirit than was possible in the now corrupted Church.

At the same time, interest in ritual magic and in all manner of psychic practices was growing. The Society for Psychical Research was founded in London in 1882 and in 1888 the Hermetic Order of the Golden Dawn was formed, its members being introduced to the kabbalah, the hermetic texts, and other arcane wisdom of the ancient world. By then, Spiritualism had been around for decades, and interest in communicating with the unseen world had grown considerably. Many of these groups and organizations attracted the attention of influential people. For instance, the Society for Psychical Research counted Gladstone, John Ruskin, and Lord Tennyson among its members, while W. B. Yeats was a member of the Golden Dawn, and Sir Arthur Conan Doyle was an enthusiastic Spiritualist.

[3] See www.theosophical-society.org.uk.

Many of the ideas and practices promoted by these groups and others have now been accepted into the mainstream, and any bookshop today will give evidence of their influence by the volume of shelf space they increasingly command. The view that the New Age movement exploded onto the scene in the 1960s does not always acknowledge the length of its gestation period, from the later half of the nineteenth century through the first half of the twentieth.

It took time, after all, to develop a spirituality so in tune with the Relativist spirit of the age, with its rejection of tradition and authority, its emphasis on individual rather than objective truth, its embracing of change and the concept of man as spiritually evolving, and its insistence that all religions are equally valid.

3. Psychoanalysis

The discovery of the unconscious gave the modern age a new celestial realm. This new unseen region was originally proposed by Sigmund Freud as the repository of repressed and usually unpleasant emotional material, which had a habit of surfacing while his patients were undergoing hypnosis. At the time when Freud's theory of the unconscious first came to light, current opinion was that once a memory was lost it was gone forever and that the mind was not capable of storing memories of which the individual was unaware.

Freud proposed that the human mind had both a conscious and an unconscious component.[4] The conscious mind was responsible for day-to-day behavior, including rational

[4] Sigmund Freud, *On Metapsychology: The Theory of Psychoanalysis* (London: Penguin Books, 1991).

thought and conversation, et cetera, while the unconscious mind, which governed bodily functions such as respiration and heart rate, also served as a repository for painful memories that could not be handled at the conscious level. While this strategy had the advantage of protecting the individual from distress, the disadvantage was that memories repressed in this way could still adversely affect behavior. Psychoanalysis, according to Freud, could bring repressed memories to the surface and heal them.

But it was Carl Jung, an early follower of Freud, whose theories were to combine so well with the ideas of the modern age. Born the only son of a Swiss Protestant pastor in 1875, he believed he was composed of two distinct personalities, which he termed No. 1 and No. 2 respectively. No. 1 was the son of his parents, who went to school and conformed to the society around him, while No. 2 was remote from the world of social norms but more in touch with the mysteries of life. He believed that his No. 2 personality gave him the advantage of direct access to God, which was denied to his father whom he came to pity for being trapped by theology and dogma.[5]

As a medical student at Basel University, for the purposes of study he attended the séances of a young medium who was also his cousin. While working for his doctorate, he developed the theory that personalities existing in the unconscious psyche can emerge during dreams, hallucinations, and trances. After training as a psychiatrist, Jung traveled to Vienna to meet Freud, and the two remained close colleagues for some years until differences of opinion arose between them.

[5] Anthony Stevens, *Jung: A Very Short Introduction* (Oxford: Oxford University Press, 1994), 8, 13, 22, 30.

Jung believed that beneath the personal unconscious of repressed wishes and traumatic memories proposed by Freud, there lay a deeper and more important layer containing the entire psychic heritage of Mankind. The figures and symbols present in dreams, myths, and fairytales originated in what he termed the collective unconscious, which was common to all mankind and from which the individual builds his own psychic life.

The publication of this and other theories of Jung's provoked a break-up with Freud that led to Jung temporarily withdrawing from the psychoanalytic establishment. During this period, he experienced a number of horrifying visions, heard voices in his head, and held conversations with imaginary companions. Two figures he regularly encountered were a beautiful young woman called Salome and an old man called Philemon who had a white beard and the wings of a kingfisher. Eventually Jung came to see these figures as the embodiment of two archetypes, the eternal feminine and the wise old man. As he emerged from this crisis, Jung began to produce drawings resembling ancient mandalas, which he believed represented the self and its psychic transformations.

Jung's work in this area developed into the idea that the mythical hero's quest is really a journey into the unconscious, where gods and monsters representing psychic forces have to be faced for the individual to become whole. This is the main task of life, according to Joseph Campbell, author of many works, including *The Hero with a Thousand Faces*, which was published in 1949 and apparently inspired George Lucas to produce the *Star Wars* series. Campbell hugely popularized the idea that the deities and personalities of the world's religions and myths are creations of the collective unconscious. God, the angels, the devil, and the Virgin Mary are therefore simply archetypes, or psychic manifestations common to mankind, the forms they take being dependent on culture and history. The journey into the unconscious could then be identified as a spiritual journey, the quest being to encounter the archetypes within.

Once the pilgrim's ultimate destination was the realm of God, which was located beyond the stars and had the theology and dogma of a revealed religion to point the way. But in a Relativist universe, the quest for understanding became a journey within, embarked upon under the guidance of the analyst. On the way to this new celestial realm, it is the experiences of the individual that matter. The journey to the new heaven is a personal one designed to encounter the archetypes, overcome their influences, and, as a result, unearth the true self and give it expression. Only by this process can the individual fully emerge from the straightjacket of repressed psychic forces and external restraints and in the process become a truly authentic person in tune with creation.

4. Neopaganism

The U.K. Pagan Federation[6] was founded in 1981 from the Pagan Front and aims to promote love and kinship with nature and its ever-renewing cycles of life and death; a morality expressed as, "Do what you will, as long as it harms none", in which the individual is responsible for the discovery and development of his true nature in harmony with the outer world; and the recognition of a spirituality that acknowledges both the female and male aspects of the divine.

[6] See www.paganfed.demon.co.uk.

Secretary of the Pagan Federation at the time of its found-
ing was Vivianne Crowley, author of *Wicca: The Old Religion in the New Age*. For Crowley, each stage of a magic
ritual corresponds to a part of the human psyche, and the
practice of magic helps the individual explore the unconscious and connect with his own divinity, which in turn
can be attuned to the divinity of nature. The aim is to trans-
form both the self and the world.[7] Because magic and ritual can unlock the secrets of the unconscious and of the
universe, the specific role of the analyst is dispensed with, if
not the theories of the unconscious as proposed by psychoanalysis. Crowley, a self-professed witch, lectures at the Jesuit
Heythrop College on the work of Jung as part of the college's Psychology of Religion course.

According to Professor Ronald Hutton of the University
of Bristol, "modern pagan witchcraft ... is the only religion which England has ever given to the world."[8] The
roots of modern pagan witchcraft lie in the nineteenth-
century tendency to react against industrialization by ide-
alizing the countryside and to look for a deeper spirituality
than could be offered by a mystery-free, post-Reformation
church.

The idea grew that the ancient religions had been marked
by a blissful union with nature and that the reforging of
this union required a rediscovery of the spirits and deities
of the pre-Christian world. As a result of the "oppressive
Church", these had been driven deep into the woods and
groves to continue their carefree dances and midsummer
revels in secret, under the watchful gaze of a country people

---

[7] Vivianne Crowley, *Wicca: The Old Religion in the New Age* (Welling-
borough, Eng.: Aquarian Books, 1989).

[8] Ronald Hutton, *The Triumph of the Moon: A History of Modern Pagan Witchcraft* (Oxford: Oxford University Press, 1999), preface, vii.

who had never fully abandoned their pagan ways. The English Folklore Society, founded in 1878, was just one source of the notion that grew among Victorian folklorists that the ancient paganism had survived the imposition of the dogmas and rituals of Christianity.

At the same time the theory that ancient peoples were matriarchal and worshipped a "Great Goddess" began to gain ground, and this belief is now fully established in neo-pagan circles. The goddess personified the reproductive energies of nature, while her son and consort, who represented the spirit of vegetation, died every autumn and returned the following spring. She was then usurped by the newer patriarchal religions, but despite centuries of oppression by the Church, her worship never died out. The old religion survived in the guise of traditional folk customs until nineteenth- and twentieth-century scholarship uncovered it and began the process of restoring the goddess to her rightful place as supreme mother of all the gods.

The argument goes on. Christianity, in common with all patriarchal religions, is an aggressive and power-hungry tradition that stole or borrowed most of its ideas from the peaceful and harmonious religions preceding it. In this light, Christ's death and Resurrection is simply another version of the dying and returning god of vegetation. Similarly the figure of the devil is a corruption of the pagan horned god. Most of the rituals of the medieval Church, it is also argued, were adaptations of pagan rituals, and medieval churches were frequently built on the sites of pagan temples.

The basic thesis put forward by Sir James Frazer in *The Golden Bough* (1890) was the predominance in pre-Christian cultures of the goddess and her dying and returning son. Dion Fortune, author of *The Goat Foot God* (1936), said that the Virgin Mary was just another aspect of the great goddess. Robert Graves in *The White Goddess* (1948) linked the three aspects of the goddess—maiden, mother, crone—to three phases of the moon, and the two aspects of her dying and returning son to the waxing and the waning of the year.

Margaret Murray, a member of the Folklore Society and author of *The Witch Cult in Western Europe* (1921) and *The God of the Witches* (1933), announced that Joan of Arc had really been a worshipper of the ancient religion. She claimed to provide evidence that the horned god of fertility was the oldest deity known to mankind and had been worshipped extensively throughout Europe in ancient times and who later became the Christian devil. It was the continued worship of this god, she said, that had inspired the Church to make accusations of witchcraft and to attempt to stamp it out with witch trials and burnings. Murray also linked medieval church carvings with surviving paganism and inspired her colleague at the Folklore Society, Lady Raglan, to claim that the foliate heads in early churches were representations of the "Green Man", or vegetation god proposed by Sir James Frazer. The first issue of the Folklore Society's periodical in 1890 stated that the legend of Lady Godiva was an example of a pagan fertility rite expropriated by the Church for her own use.

The new pagans have begun to reclaim Church festivals. Christmas can now double up as a midwinter festival; Easter is also a celebration of renewal associated with the spring equinox; and Halloween should be remembered not as the Eve of All Saints' Day, but as the day on which the Druids honored their dead and appeased their gods. It must be particularly satisfying for these neopagans to watch as the Church adopts pagan imagery into her buildings, such as the aptly nicknamed "Horns of Hathor" in Armagh Cathedral, and the far too common rough-hewn altars that resemble something the Aztecs would have used.

The theme of the persecution of pagans as the real motive behind the witch trials was later taken up by mainly American feminist authors such as Andrea Dworkin and Mary Daly. The women put to death during the "Burning Times" were really practitioners of the old religion, wise women and healers who worked for the benefit of their communities. It was now up to the feminist movement to liberate women from the yoke of destructive patriarchal oppression and to rediscover the "witch within" by returning to the goddess and embracing her power.

To what extent neopaganism is inspired by the spirit of the age can be partly deduced from its portrayal of Christianity as derivative and owing many of its practices to the far older and wiser religions of the ancients. While it is true that Christianity "baptized" what could be redeemed in paganism, as in those symbols and practices that pointed to Christ, the argument that the Church has simply stolen her traditions from people she oppressed is an attempt to diminish the status of Christianity. Theosophy, which states that all religions are equally valid interpretations of the great universal spirit, and Jungian psychoanalysis, which represents the deities of the world religions as mere personifications of forces present in the collective unconscious, also deny the unique salvific role the Church claims for Christ.

Neopaganism points to a golden age lost in the mists of time and seeks to restore it to its former glory, the main opposition to this being the Church. That the monotheistic religions of the West are products of a male revolt against the goddess in particular and women in general, forms the basis of the argument here, but this yearning for a lost arcadia is also a feature of a number of Modernist ideas. It expresses itself in the outright dismissal of centuries of Western tradition and the call to start again. For the neopagans, the best of times existed before the rise of the patriarchal and monotheistic religions, specifically Christianity, and their particular favorites are the Druids and the builders of stone circles. The Theosophists are not so specific, but many claim the golden age to have been represented by the lost civilization of Atlantis, if it ever indeed existed. And the Jungians, while agreeing that Western culture is corrupt, point to a new enlightenment that will come as soon as everyone realizes that salvation is to be found via the inner road of the unconscious.

They all agree that the two preceding millennia of Christianity ought to be forgotten as quickly as possible, and modernizers in the Church have also embraced this opinion. The time scale might be different, with the golden age being identified as the time of the early Church, before centuries of dogma and tradition confounded it.

5. Evolution

Since most people are familiar with evolutionary theory as presented by Darwin and subsequent generations of scientists, it is more useful here to examine the evolutionary world view arising from the theory, a view proposing that reality exists only in movement, that nothing is fixed, and everything is in a state of flux. The evolutionary outlook promotes *becoming* rather than *being*, and *motion* rather than *rest*. It also values the act over the product of the act, the fact that something is taking place being considered of greater significance than its outcome.

Nothing is free from change, since nothing can be judged to have an absolute value. Liturgical experiments are intrinsically good, not because they may involve the improvement of doubtful practices or the elimination of abuses, but for their own sake, because the liturgy, like everything else, is constantly evolving. Therefore if the position of the baptismal font in today's churches changes as frequently as the fashion in shoes, then this is not an indication of contemporary disorientation. Instead it demonstrates that the People of God have made a significant step toward realizing their creativity. A living Church is a creative Church, a dynamic Church.

Constant change is desirable because the end result will inevitably be better than the starting point. The idea that creation in general and mankind in particular is evolving, is in direct contrast to the Fall. It is difficult to see how the traditional view that mankind fell from an original state of grace and had to be saved by the sacrifice of a divine Redeemer, can sit easily with the idea that mankind is constantly evolving, because to evolve means always to achieve a higher and better state. Species that fail to adapt to changing circumstances will always die out.

Nevertheless, according to the evolutionary view, both mankind and human society are constantly improving and moving forward. As James Hitchcock points out in *The Decline and Fall of Radical Catholicism*,

> a good deal of contemporary radical thought is based on a dogma which is not even recognised as such, a highly dubious speculation which is taken as certainty—that the human race is undergoing a profound transformation which will eliminate the need for law, tradition, authority and duty, that men of the future will live as totally spontaneous beings guided only by their inner promptings

and their concern for others and capable of freely will-
ing and creating a world immensely superior to any yet
seen.[9]

It therefore follows that any habit, custom, or tradition
left over from a less enlightened age and deemed to be no
longer fit for the present must be rejected. Those who prefer the established ways and wish to retain them are classed
as obstacles to progress, fit only to be ignored, deserving of
derision for clinging to the past, and accused of being reac-
tionary, conservative, and frightened of the future, terms
frequently applied to groups and individuals both inside and
outside the Church who resist a change they anticipate will
be for the worse.

6. Revolution

While evolutionists are prepared to accept gradual, continual change and will view history as a process of slow and
sometimes imperceptible progress, those who hold a revolutionary world view tend not to be so patient. History
and mankind might be heading toward a new and golden
future, but the great upheavals along the way keep the process moving and on course.

It was the nineteenth-century German philosopher Hegel
who claimed that human history strives toward the perfect
state through the dialectic process, which involves an existing set of ideas being challenged by a set of opposing ideas
until, in the ensuing struggle, new and dominant ideas
emerge. And since the truths, morals, and concepts held by
one society are overthrown by those of the society succeeding

[9] James Hitchcock, *The Decline and Fall of Radical Catholicism* (New York:
Image Books, Doubleday, 1972), 100.

it, a particular body of thought is only relevant to the society that once held it.

Then the Marxists took the dialectical process Hegel had claimed was at work in the realm of ideas, applied it to social and economic forces, and gave the world the concept of dialectical materialism so loved in revolutionary circles. It was changing economic conditions, such as the rise of a merchant class to challenge the power of the old aristocracy, that had brought about the end of feudalism and the Middle Ages. As capitalism developed and a new bourgeoisie began to create the industrial society, a proletariat had emerged that would eventually overthrow capitalism and create a classless socialist society in which the state, as the instrument of the dominant class, would wither away.

Most twentieth-century revolutionaries came from the educated middle-class, and although they disapproved of the lingering but much diminished power of the old aristocracy, their dislike of everything capitalist and bourgeois was matched only by their contempt for those among the masses who refused to side with them. The masses were the very people they were trying to liberate from their chains, to free from their oppression. It simply was not permissible for them to refuse this offer.

The revolutionary view prefers youth to age, and there is hardly a revolutionary movement of the twentieth century that did not make a specific point of enlisting the young to help overthrow the established order, including Stalin's Young Communist League; the youthful perpetrators of Chairman Mao's cultural revolution who forced university professors to work in the paddy fields; and the Khmer Rouge, who, with an average age of twenty-one, acted on the instructions of Pol Pot to eliminate the entire professional class of Cambodia, thereby murdering two million people.

"Out with the old and in with the new" has been the rallying cry of many a modern movement seeking to demolish an existing way of doing things and replace it with a new. It is one of the tactics of moderns to jettison the past, thereby justifying the radical changes being proposed for, and frequently imposed on, people who are both unaware of being oppressed and unenthusiastic about the changes. The leaders of the 1960s sexual revolution did this, by claiming that everyone who had lived previously had been repressed, narrow-minded, and bigoted. How better to herald the dawn of a new era than by denouncing the past as worthy only of being swept away? "Starting from zero" was a favorite slogan of Pol Pot, who was educated in Paris. But it had already been said, decades before.

3

The Architecture of Relativist Space

Starting from zero was one of the big ideas at the Bauhaus school of design in Weimar, Germany, founded in 1919 by the architect Walter Gropius. Starting from zero was necessary to create a pure, new architecture for a pure, new future. Many of the prophets of Modernism taught at the Bauhaus—Ludwig Mies van der Rohe, László Moholy-Nagy, and Henry van de Velde—not to mention the artist Paul Klee, who nicknamed Gropius "the Silver Prince", and Wassily Kandinsky.

The origins of the modern movement in architecture, in which the Bauhaus played a fundamental role, can be traced back to the last years of the nineteenth century. In 1897, in Vienna, a group of artists and architects separated themselves from the Austrian art establishment and formed the "Vienna Secession", thereby creating the first of the art compounds that were to change the face of world architecture.

Typically the members of an art compound—whether they be Constructivists, Neoplasticists, or Elementarists—would form an artistic community by meeting regularly, agreeing on certain aesthetic and moral principles and then publicizing them, usually in the form of a manifesto. The Italian Futurists delivered their first manifesto in 1910. After that the manifestos hardly stopped coming, with the De Stijl group producing theirs in 1918. Before the First World War, the Deutsche Werkbund, where Gropius had been a leading figure, had already set about designing the perfect forms of architecture and art for all of Germany. After the war, the various compounds competed with one another to produce the most pure architectural vision for the future. In 1922, the First International Congress of Progressive Art was held in Düsseldorf, and 1923 was the year of the first Bauhaus exhibition.

It was agreed by all that the traditions were obsolete, the styles redundant, and all forms of embellishment and decoration should be rejected. Instead what was required was a revolutionary and universal architectural aesthetic to be found through geometry, mass production, and the use of honestly expressed materials. This meant that color was out, or at

I
Bauhaus school of design, Dessau, 1925–26.
Architect—Walter Gropius.

least any color apart from beige and gray and, of course, black and white. Pitched roofs, it had been decided, represented the crowns of the old nobility and so flat roofs became compulsory, despite the climate and the consequent fact that so many of them leaked. Eaves and cornices also had to be eliminated so that the roof could make a clean right angle with the building façade. And above all, nothing should be covered up, nothing should be hidden. From henceforth the structure of the building had to *show*.

The architect Le Corbusier was to produce one of the twentieth century's most influential works of architectural theory. His designs for workers' housing were the inspiration for the estates of later decades, and here the spatial principles underling them were laid out. The past was dead and the future was wide open, as he observed in *Towards a New Architecture*: "A great epoch has begun. There exists a new spirit. Architecture is stifled by custom. The 'styles' are a lie." [1]

Just as relativity had helped free universal space from the absolutes, so architectural space was liberated from traditional concepts. New construction methods employing steel and reinforced concrete allowed greater spans to be achieved without so much solid masonry. Space could now "flow" because there was no longer any need to restrict an activity to an area enclosed by heavy walls. Sliding doors and partitions would allow activity areas, or zones, to be closed off and opened up again as the need arose.

Buildings were no longer to be considered in terms of connected but individually defined *spaces*, but as an expression of unbounded, nonhierarchical *space*, space that could be multifunctional and flexible because nothing need be

[1] Le Corbusier, *Towards a New Architecture* (1946; London: Architectural Press, repr. 1976), 82.

2
Postcard of the Weissenhof Estate, Stuttgart, 1927.

fixed or absolute. The old formalities were lifted; the boundaries were dissolved; open plan was born. Lightweight cur-
tain walling and extensive areas of glazing would help lighten
the perimeters of buildings and visually connect their interiors with the landscape. Raising buildings off the ground
on columns, or "piloti", would allow the space around them
to flow without restriction or limitation. Abandoning the
traditional patterns of streets, squares, avenues, courtyards,
and so forth would liberate the city, and buildings would
no longer need to fit into an imposed ground plan.

The new vision was intended for the benefit of the masses,
and if the masses were slow to catch on, they would have
to be reeducated. It was only to be expected that most people
would lag behind the visionaries and be slow to appreciate
the wonders of what was offered. But it mattered little anyway:

the patronage of mostly socialist town and city authorities would put money behind the new architecture and make the vision a reality. Then the eyes of the people would be opened by the experience of living the dream, and the work of building new cities for a new future could begin in earnest. The fact that this meant demolishing large parts of existing cities was no matter for regret. Nothing was to be spared. The time had come to brush aside the dead hand of the past.

The trouble was, the masses would not cooperate. They were far too stubborn, too set in their ways, to appreciate their new housing with its flat roofs and sheer walls with no window architraves or raised lintels. They took one look at their pure white interiors, purged of all casings, cornices, covings, crown moldings, et cetera, and their open-plan layouts that gave them no privacy and began to introduce curtains, wallpaper, lamps with fringed shades, upholstered furniture, ornaments, and flowery carpets. The architectural visionaries complained, but their ideas had been sold. The middle decades of the twentieth century saw the new city being built over most of the globe.

The new town and city planners had no qualms about eradicating street patterns that had developed over centuries, or demolishing entire neighborhoods that, over successive generations, had established complex support systems and intricate relationships. Armed with their felt-tipped pens, the planners would boldly circle an area on a map and designate it as "Scheduled for Redevelopment", a term that would come to strike fear into the hearts of town- and city-dwellers, just as the notice "Scheduled for Reordering" would eventually come to be viewed with dread by the laity at the local church.

As the decades wore on, the fashion for the plain white box began to change. There were attempts to demonstrate the poetic qualities of bulky concrete structures in which the only form of enhancement permitted were the shuttering marks created by the timber cases into which the concrete had been poured. Some architects even dared to experiment with brickwork, to soften the image of their designs and offer a concession to its inhabitants. But the ideas about space remained. Space had to be free-flowing and unbounded: no gradations or hierarchies were permitted. Great blocks of mass-produced housing units were laid out without any particular plan at all, other than what was considered to be most functional for the site. Private and semiprivate space was kept to an absolute minimum because these require boundaries. The creation of universal space was the aim.

But still the masses refused to cooperate, and resistance to the new vision grew exponentially. By the late '70s and early '80s the architects themselves could only agree that Modernist ideas about space had created an entirely unacceptable urban environment. Ultimately, it was on the issue of Relativist space that the argument turned.

* * *

Throughout the early twentieth century, elemental purity was sought in primary geometric forms—the circle, square, and triangle, and in primary colors—red, blue, and yellow. Modernist artists believed in the universality of these forms and that paring everything down to these basic elements would release universal truth.

Searching for the underlying essence of things has been a serious undertaking in the modern age. A set of monochrome canvases takes on new significance if they are really a meditation on the theme of, say, yellow. A single note played by a symphony orchestra becomes a contemplation of that one sound, a study on that one note. Colors and sounds have vibrations, and by tuning into them their truth can be known. Forms also have vibrations, according to those who sit cross-legged inside pyramids at mind-body-and-spirit festivals.

The dematerializing of the arts and the dissolving of the boundaries between them was evidence that a new epoch was dawning, according to Kandinsky, who cited as evidence Matisse's freeing of color and Picasso's decomposition of the solid form. The aim was to shatter the forms completely and merge them into one another. Plastic art and plastic architecture were the aim. Nothing is fixed, nothing permanent. A truly International Style, a universal architecture, would transcend both historical style and regional conditions. Space, light, color, sound, and materials could then express the one underlying truth that unites everything.

During the search for what underlies everything, the appearances were discarded. A homogenous universe found its expression in a homogenous architecture. Modernism was trumpeted as the style for a new dawn, the new epoch that had begun. The impulse was to strip everything away, to discard the superfluous, dispense with the trappings. Only what was left would have any meaning. In his critique of Modernist architecture, *From Bauhaus to Our House*, Tom Wolfe comments:

> So what if you were living in a building that looked like a factory and felt like a factory, and paying top dollar for it? Every modern building of quality looked like a factory. That was the *look of today*. You only had to think of Mies' campus for the Illinois Institute of Technology, most of which had gone up in the 1940s. The main classroom

building looked like a shoe factory. The chapel looked like a power plant. The power plant itself, also designed by Mies, looked rather more spiritual (as Charles Jencks would point out), thanks to its chimney, which reached heavenward at least. The school of architecture building had black steel trusses rising up through the roof on either side of the main entrance, after the manner of a Los Angeles car wash. All four were glass and steel boxes. The truth was, this was inescapable. The compound style, with its *nonbourgeois* taboos, had so reduced the options of the true believer that every building, the beach house no less than the skyscraper, was bound to have the same general look.[2]

Modernism attempted to create a radically new architecture that would embody the principles of Relativist space in built form. Liberation from the clutter of the past was the aim, with the promise of an uncompromising and vital new future, a future in which meaning would be revealed by dispensing with unnecessary accumulations. The pioneers of the International Style predicted the dawning of a new epoch dedicated to universal truth. However the sun rose on the Birmingham Bullring and the Peckham Estate, both of which have been demolished, along with so many Modernist visions of the future.

According to the visionaries, Modernism was the style for the machine age. Rational, functional, and aesthetically unhampered, it was the honest and scientific response to contemporary needs. However, recent research suggests that there was a spiritual agenda behind the modern movement

[2] Tom Wolfe, *From Bauhaus to Our House* (London: Abacus, 1983), 72. Published in the U.K. by Jonathan Cape (1982). Published in the U.S.A. by Farrar, Straus and Giroux, 1981.

in art and architecture. This research builds on the work of architectural historian Joseph Rykwert, who in 1968 published a paper titled "The Dark Side of the Bauhaus", in which he discusses how far the ideas promoted by the Theosophical societies in Europe influenced the architects at the Bauhaus and the painters and sculptors of the decades before the First World War.

> I hope that I will not risk paradox if I now accuse the Bauhaus masters—not of an excessive rationalism—but rather of not stating the religious, or quasi-religious postulates for what they were doing; or at any rate of not stating them explicitly. Only Itten and Klee have a clean record in this respect: and they were the two Bauhaus masters who realised most clearly the danger of van Doesburg's excessive devotion to modernity; to interpreting every technological advance as a spiritual leap forward.[3]

Architronic, the electronic journal of architecture, has recently devoted an entire issue to examining the influence of Theosophy on the pioneers of the Modernist style.

> As Rykwert observed in 1968, a strong current of occult and mystical thought, Gustav Pehnt's "non-religious religiousness", permeated much of modernist discourse at the turn of the century. The Expressionists, with whom we generally associate such esoteric predilections, produced works ranging from the crystalline utopias of Taut and Scheerbart, to the exotic practices of Johannes Itten in the *Vorkurs'* of the Bauhaus, to dark, racial and nationalist theories reflected in the works of Bernhard Hoetger. Esotericism also formed a strain within the ranks of

[3] Joseph Rykwert, "The Dark Side of the Bauhaus", in *The Necessity of Artifice: Ideas in Architecture* (London: Academy Editions, 1982), 49.

3
National Congress, Brasilia, Brazil, 1956–60.
Architect—Oscar Niemeyer.

the avant garde. Malevich, Mondrian, van Doesburg and El Lissitzky were some of those who found the key to an alternative modernity in esoteric thought. Their manifestos and declarations, colored by the pursuit of the non-objective world, proclaimed the arrival of Vorticism, Suprematism, Neo-Plasticism, Futurism and Elementarism in turn.[4]

That the promoters of the Modernist style had a spiritual agenda will barely be mentioned in the writings of most twentieth-century art and architecture critics. It is an agenda that would certainly explain many of the characteristics of the Modernist style and the approach of its proponents. Firstly, there is the desire to dismiss two millennia of accumulated knowledge and practice at a stroke. Secondly, there is the desire to recapture a long-gone age of elemental purity—modern artists have always been in love with primitivism and modern architects with the mastery of geometry displayed by the Greeks, the Egyptians, the Incas. It is part of being modern, to emulate the most ancient building forms.

Thirdly, there is the announcing of a new future that only the enlightened and those in the know can appreciate and understand, coupled with calls for the reeducation of the ignorant and the reluctant. This has been a characteristic of revolutionary movements throughout the modern age, the aim of a revolution being to dismantle the hierarchies, dissolve the boundaries, and eliminate the divisions. Every point of view is valid in the new world being fought for, except the opinion of those—the reactionaries—who reject the vision and who, it is anticipated, will die out as the "new man" is born.

[4] Susan R. Henderson, "Architecture and Theosophy: An Introduction", *Architronic Magazine* 8, no. 1 (January 1999), http://architronic.saed.kent.edu/.

The Modernist style of architecture dominated church design throughout the latter half of the twentieth century. Recently, the aesthetics may have softened, but the ideas about space informing the style remain the same, with the result that churches continue to be constructed according to principles of Relativist space, principles that have already been found wanting in the secular world.

4

The Relativist Church Building

One of the complaints people often make about modern church buildings is that they do not look like churches. In some quarters this may be seen as evidence of a sentimental attachment to outmoded concepts, provoking a response such as, "But we've been freed from the limitations of traditional forms, so who's to say what a church should look like?"

This is the kind of question that invites only one answer—nobody. It is an opinion that is likely to be followed by the claim, mentioned earlier, that church architecture has always changed from age to age, and that since a Baroque church looks different from a medieval church, modern churches are following the example of the past by reflecting the architectural ideas of today. Another response to the dismay many feel at the state of contemporary church architecture admits that it does represent a departure from the past and, indeed, may not always be beautiful but claims the style of new churches reflects the ideas of the Second Vatican Council, and therefore it is the "mind of the Church" that churches today should look as they do.

Some commentators on the documents of Vatican II insist that the Council did not mandate the changes that have taken place to the Church's buildings and liturgy. Others maintain that in order to understand the will of the Council fully, reference also has to be made to the *post*conciliar documents, particularly *Cenam Paschalem* or the *General*

Instruction on the Roman Missal (GIRM) (March 26, 1970). While it is not possible here to cover all the arguments for and against these claims, it is useful to have a look at some of them. For example, Michael Davies in *The Catholic Sanctuary and the Second Vatican Council* draws attention to the directives spelled out in *Sacrosanctum Concilium*, the Council's *Constitution on the Sacred Liturgy* (December 4, 1963):

> The Liturgy Constitution contained stipulations which appeared to rule out the least possibility of any drastic remodelling of the traditional Mass or the sanctuaries in which it was celebrated. The Latin language was to be preserved in the Latin rites (Article 36), and steps were to be taken to ensure that the faithful could sing or say together in Latin those parts of the Mass that pertain to them (Article 54). All lawfully acknowledged rites were held to be of equal authority and dignity and were to be preserved in the future and fostered in every way (Article 4). The treasury of sacred music was to be preserved and fostered with great care (Article 114) and Gregorian chant was to be given pride of place in liturgical services (Article 116).[1]

Later on Michael Davies also states:

> The rubrics of the New Mass, approved specifically by Pope Paul VI, presume that the priest will be facing the altar in the traditional manner as the norm for its celebration. The rubrics of the 1970 Missal instruct the priest to turn to the congregation at specific moments of the Mass and then turn back to face the altar. These rubrics can also be found in the General Instruction, Articles 107, 115, 116, 122, 198 and 199. Where the

---

[1] Michael Davies, *The Catholic Sanctuary and the Second Vatican Council* (Rockford, Ill.: Tan Books, 1997), 17.

rubrics governing the actual celebration of Mass are concerned, both in the Order of Mass and in the General Instruction, *there is not one which envisages a celebration facing the people!*[2]

To check these points, then, it should be enough to consult what is considered an authoritative translation of the pronouncements of the Council—*Vatican Council II:The Conciliar and Post Conciliar Documents*, edited by Austin Flannery, O.P.[3] And sure enough, article 36 of *Sacrosanctum Concilium* definitely does state, "The use of the Latin language, with due respect to particular law, is to be preserved in the Latin rites"; article 54 does say, "care must be taken to ensure that the faithful may also be able to say or sing together in Latin those parts of the Ordinary of the Mass which pertain to them"; article 4 says, "in faithful obedience to tradition, the sacred Council declares that Holy Mother Church holds all lawfully recognised rites to be of equal right and dignity"; article 114 says, "The treasury of sacred music is to be cultivated with great care"; and according to article 116, "The Church recognises Gregorian chant as being specially suited to the Roman liturgy. Therefore, other things being equal, it should be given pride of place in liturgical services."

However, in order to check Michael Davies' claim that, "The rubrics of the 1970 Missal instruct the priest to turn to the congregation at specific moments of the Mass and then turn back to face the altar", it is necessary to consult the relevant articles in the *General Instruction on the Roman Missal* (GIRM). But these are not reproduced in full in the Austin Flannery translation.

[2] Ibid., 26.

[3] Austin Flannery, O.P., *Vatican Council II: The Conciliar and Postconciliar Documents* (Dublin: Dominican Publications, 1992; Northpoint, N.Y.: Costello Publishing Co.).

To find the missing articles, then, it is necessary to consult a 1973 translation of the GIRM published by the Catholic Truth Society.[4] According to this version, paragraph 107 states, "Returning to the middle of the altar the priest, facing the people, extends and then joins his hands, while inviting the people to pray, saying: 'Pray, brethren . . .' etc." Paragraph 115 also states, "Having finished the prayer the priest genuflects, picks up the host, raises it slightly above the paten and, facing the people, says: 'This is the Lamb of God.' " But then, according to paragraph 116, "facing the altar, he [the priest] says inaudibly: 'May the body of Christ bring me to everlasting life. . . .' " And paragraph 122 states, "After this the priest standing at his chair or else at the altar, facing the people, says: 'Let us pray.' " Here, at least, is evidence that according to the full text of the GIRM, the priest should generally be facing the altar and then should turn to face the people at certain points throughout the Mass.

The later paragraphs contain instructions referring to concelebrated Masses. According to paragraph 198, "The principle celebrant takes a host, holds it a little above the paten and says, facing the people: 'Behold the Lamb of God. . . .' " Then, as paragraph 199 states, "the principle celebrant, facing the altar, says softly: 'May the body of Christ bring me to everlasting life.' The concelebrants do the same."

As has already been pointed out, these paragraphs do not appear in the Austin Flannery translation, the very paragraphs suggesting that the New Mass is intended to be said as it has always been said, with the priest and people facing the same direction. His reason for leaving them out is "Nn.

---

[4] *General Instruction on the Roman Missal*, trans. Clifford Howell, S.J. (London: Catholic Truth Society, 1973).

77 to 141, inclusive are omitted: they are detailed directives on the celebration of Mass." And similarly, "Nn. 159 to 239, inclusive, are omitted: they are detailed directives on the celebration of the Mass."

Admittedly article 262 of the GIRM states, "Normally a church should have a fixed and dedicated altar, freestanding, away from the wall, so that the priest can walk all around it and can celebrate facing the people. . . ." This brief mention of the "facing the people" orientation is thus the justification for the reordering of church sanctuaries across the world, while the paragraphs indicating that the traditional priestly orientation is to be retained in the New Mass are ignored.

Of course almost anything written can be interpreted in different ways, although the above statements seem quite clear in their differentiation between the orientation of the priest facing the congregation and facing the altar. The answer to the question of whether Vatican II actually mandated the whole-scale adoption of the *versus populum* orientation depends on who is asked. Those against the change will say no and point to the wording of the Council documents. Those in favor of the change will say yes, pointing to its brief mention in article 262, and then invoke the "spirit of Vatican II".

That the twentieth-century revolution in church architecture cannot be considered separately from the revolution in the Church's liturgy is admitted by the promoters of the revolution themselves, who insist that a new church building is required for a new liturgy. Yet at the same time they also insist that the New Mass is only the latest in a series of reforms to the liturgy instigated by previous popes. And so just as Pope Pius V promulgated the *Missale Romanum* in 1570, following the Council of Trent, so did Pope Paul VI promulgate the Missal of 1970, following the Second Vatican Council. But according to the GIRM, paragraph 7, "In point of fact the Missal of 1570 differs very little indeed from the first Missal which dates from the year 1474, and this in turn follows very closely a Mass book dated back to the time of Pope Innocent III." In other words, Pope Pius V did not promulgate a new Order of Mass, whereas Pope Paul VI did.

The call for liturgical renewal predates Vatican II, with the first half of the twentieth century producing an abundance of scholarship on the liturgy. The period after World War I saw the rise of the "dialogue Mass" in Germany, beginning in academic circles and youth groups and then spreading to the parishes. During this form of the low Mass, the congregation would say out loud the responses previously recited in a low voice by the acolyte. By the 1950s, the "dialogue Mass" had spread to the United States, where it became the form adopted by self-styled liturgical "progressives". Similarly, the celebration of Mass facing the people was not unknown before Vatican II, having already been adopted in "progressive" liturgical circles and youth groups, again in Germany.

The early twentieth century also saw the development of the Liturgical Movement, which had among its aims the encouragement of a greater knowledge of the liturgy among the faithful, the more widespread use of the Divine Office as a form of public prayer for the whole Church, and the study of both the teachings of the Church Fathers and the liturgies of the Eastern Orthodox churches. To this end, the first complete Latin-English missal was published in 1910—bilingual missals for the laity having been forbidden until 1897—and many of the new missals included translations of Hours of the Office for use in parishes. Another characteristic of the Liturgical Movement was its effort to promote the use of sacred music, particularly Gregorian chant, in parishes. Many of the popular, newly published missals included a considerable amount of Gregorian chant for this purpose.

That the Vatican Council heralded a liturgical and an architectural revolution that went far beyond the original aims of the Liturgical Movement is sometimes attributed to the presence of squads of liturgical experts, the "*periti*", who held a separate council in the cafes and restaurants around the Vatican and used their influence to push their own agenda through the Council and throughout the postconciliar period. The most active of these liturgical experts seem to have been the advisors to the so-called "Rhine Group", bishops from mainly Germany, Holland, and parts of France.

Overwhelmingly of a liberal persuasion, this group has been described as going into action from the very start of the Council by forming pressure groups to lobby for the advancement of their ideas and attempting to gain control of the Council's ten commissions. As the Council progressed, their influence grew, it has been said, and the English-speaking bishops in particular began to accept their ideas. During the postconciliar period the work of advancing the reforms continued, through the use of the press and other media, which welcomed and promoted almost any and every proposal to tear down existing structures and overthrow tradition.

Many of these changes, not being proposed in the actual Council documents, were instigated in the "spirit of Vatican II". There can be no denying that they have altered the face of Catholicism throughout the world and produced the ugliest churches in history. It is far beyond the scope of this discussion to be concerned with anything more

than the briefest look at a tiny portion of Council documents, sometimes referred to as the "letter of Vatican II",
as opposed to the "spirit of Vatican II". This is a useful
distinction, the "spirit of Vatican II" being none other than
the spirit of the age, which is the spirit of Relativism—or
at least that is the proposal here.

Besides, there is no real need to rely on the documents
and arguments mentioned above to detect the actions and
effects of this spirit (although since such a wealth of scholarship has been devoted to uncovering its real nature, it
would be a shame not to study this body of work). All that
is really necessary is to look at the results, among them the
contemporary church building, which so blatantly announces
the spirit of the age at work.

A member of the Catholic Bishops' Conference of England
and Wales once said, "A church is not a sacred building as
such. Instead it is rendered sacred by the liturgical action of
the people." Such a view could have come straight out of
Architecture for Worship by E. A. Sovik, who has been described
as the darling of 1960s and '70s liturgical design consultants. The ideas of this Lutheran architect have influenced
the design and reordering of countless Catholic churches
across the world and were incorporated wholeheartedly into
Environment and Art in Catholic Worship, a document released
in 1978 as a provisional draft statement by the U.S. Bishops'
Committee on the Liturgy, but in the name of the U.S.
Conference of Catholic Bishops, thereby implying the
approval of the Holy See.

Both works put forward the case for dismantling the traditional church form and replacing it with the Relativist
church building. In line with the Modernist principle of
looking back to the earliest and most ancient age possible,
Sovik consults the New Testament, where he finds no specific

mention of the first Christians either building churches or having the desire to build them. Because they recognized that wherever they were, God was, he claims, the Christians of the apostolic age met in locations most convenient for them and not in places specially aside for worship.

Developing the theme that the first Christians had no need for churches and as a result experienced a joyous and unsullied sense of community until Church bureaucracy took over and began to build the edifices we are still stuck with today, Sovik wonders if it is possible for the congregations of America to give up their ecclesiastical prejudices and be persuaded that sixteen hundred years of church building tradition could have been in error. He worries that American church people will try to settle on compromise if they are swayed away from ecclesiasticism at all, a compromise resulting in a lot of "lukewarm nothingness".

Sovik is obviously aware that most people will remain attached to their traditional church buildings and will resist the changes he is proposing. Obviously they will need to be educated out of their prejudices, like the masses anywhere who are so often unimpressed by the bold new ideas of the revolutionaries. He explains his vision thus:

> The reflections on sacramental theology have brought us back to liturgical patterns which are nearer to those of the early church.... A house of worship is not a shelter for an altar; it is a shelter for people. It is not the table that makes the sacrament; it is the people and what they do. The things are adjuncts, conveniences, symbols, utensils. The presence of God is not assured by things or by symbols or by buildings, but by Christian people.[5]

[5] E. A. Sovik, *Architecture for Worship* (Minneapolis: Augsburg Fortress Publishing House, 1973), 32–33.

One of Sovik's big new ideas is the "Non-Church", which he calls a "centrum", just in case people are confused into thinking of the building in outdated terms—in other words, in case they mistake it for a church. Although primarily concerned with the design of new "non-church" buildings, Sovik also gives examples of the kind of renewal of existing churches he would like to encourage in order to turn them into "non-church" buildings too. One example he gives is Gethsemani Abbey in Kentucky where the monks decided to "renew" the abbey church, a century-old structure with a lofty and elaborately decorated plaster-vaulted interior. By "courageously and doubtless painfully" stripping out the "contrived" gothic lining, which was only "stage-scenery" after all, the monks revealed "a noble space as elegant as it is simple" into which they moved some "well-designed new chairs" and new liturgical furnishings. According to Sovik, the result is a "sparse but beautiful room", where "people are seen as important", and where "the texture and scale of surfaces and furnishings make it hospitable and full of hope".

Environment and Art in Catholic Worship, produced by the U.S. Bishops' Committee on the Liturgy,[6] rapidly became the manual of the new breed of liturgical design consultants who were charged with advising the reordering of existing church buildings and the construction of new ones. According to paragraph 53 of *EACW*, "the entire liturgical space ... should communicate integrity (a sense of oneness, of wholeness) and a sense of being the gathering place of the initiated community."

[6] The United States Bishops' Committee on the Liturgy, *Environment and Art in Catholic Worship* (1978).

According to paragraph 72, the "holy table" should be designed for the "action of the community"; and according to paragraph 68, one is to aim for "a seating pattern and furniture pattern that . . . encourage [people] to move around when it is appropriate."

Aside from the recommendation that symbols and imagery be removed or omitted, that flexibility and multifunctional uses be accommodated, and the altar be located so that the people can "gather round", what is very telling is the suggestion that church designers aim for the creation of liturgical space that communicates "wholeness" and "oneness". Whatever can that mean, if not the creation of Relativist space that is homogenous, directionless, and value-free, thereby mirroring the spatial principles of the Relativist universe promulgated by the modern age?

These ideas also found their expression in *The Parish Church: Principles of Liturgical Design and Re-ordering*, produced by the Bishops' Conference of England and Wales.[7] Again the dismantling of the traditional church form, described in paragraph 47, is proposed. "Prior to the Second Vatican Council, a church was clearly articulated into its various parts; narthex, baptistry, nave and finally the sanctuary as the richest in decoration and set apart by rails and frequently an arch or other visual distinction. The sacristy would be adjacent to the sanctuary for direct access."

But this has to change because according to paragraph 49,

It is important, then, that a new church should be designed according to the mind of the Church which is expressed in the Constitution on the Sacred Liturgy of the Second Vatican Council, and elaborated in the subsequent

[7] The Bishops' Conference of England and Wales, *The Parish Church: Principles of Liturgical Design and Re-ordering* (London: Catholic Truth Society, 1984).

Instructions for putting the Constitution into effect. It is the task of the bishop, assisted by expert opinion, to ensure that a new church conforms to the criteria laid down in these documents.

According to paragraph 53, "The purpose of a church is to gather together the community, both priest and people, so that the Mass may be offered with the full and active participation of all who are present and, in fulfilling that role, it becomes a sign of the whole Church."

To this end, each element within the church is examined, both in the context of new design and the reordering of existing church buildings. The sanctuary should be clearly distinguished from the place of assembly (which used to be called the nave) but not so as to seem remote. To achieve greater visibility, the floor level of the sanctuary need only be one step above that of the place of assembly, and altar rails, arches, and screens can be removed so that the people are able to see the celebrant clearly. The altar itself should be free-standing since the practice of Mass facing the people is taken for granted, and it should be of a simple and uncluttered design. Seating should be arranged so that the people can gather round, preferably on chairs which both emphasize individuality and allow for greater flexibility. The aim is to achieve sparseness and avoid unnecessary elaboration. There should only be one crucifix, one altar, and one tabernacle. Furnishings should be plain and simple, and statues should be tasteful.

In 2000, the U.S. Conference of Catholic Bishops published *Built of Living Stones*, which is intended to build on and replace *EACW*. In an article for *Sacred Architecture* (the journal of the Institute of Sacred Architecture, Notre Dame University, Illinois), Timothy V. Vaverek offers a critique of *BLS* that questions this whole approach to church design, going so far as to claim that by working from the assumption that liturgy is primarily the worship of a particular community in which the presence of God is manifested and that the church building is an image of that community, *BLS* not only fails to reflect Catholic tradition adequately, it also fails to consider the centrality of the Pasch of Christ in the Church and her liturgy.[8]

Referring to various Vatican II documents, including *Sacrosanctum Concilium*, *Lumen Gentium*, and the *Rite of Dedication of a Church and Altar*, Vaverek claims that the church building "should reflect the mystery of the Church which is the communion of God and humanity wrought through the Paschal Mystery of Christ's death, resurrection and ascension. . . . The entire building is therefore 'sacramental', in that it visibly represents the Church, the Kingdom of God present now in mystery."

According to Vaverek, the current emphasis on designing church buildings that first and foremost represent the ritual worship of the community that happens to be present, fails to take account both of the full paschal life of the Church and of those members of the community not present there and then. Furthermore Vaverek asks how it can be possible to achieve the "full, conscious, and active participation" sought by Vatican II when the current theology of the liturgy is so heavily tilted toward taking part in the performance of the rites rather than more fully participating in the Paschal Mystery they signify.

Thus, to summarize the characteristics of the modern church building before going on to look at some examples.

---

[8] Rev. Timothy V. Vaverek, S.T.D., "The Church Building and Participation in the Paschal Mystery: Assessing the NCCB Document Built of Living Stones", *Sacred Architecture*, vol. 5 (2001).

—The typical Relativist church has been emptied of all but the most obscure of Catholic symbolism and imagery and presents a bland face to the world, indistinguishable from other faiths (and even from secular buildings). When the church building is intended to make an impact, say, for a cathedral or other prestigious project, any shape will do—pyramid, spiral, wigwam, giant clam—provided it does not say "church". The message is "There's nothing specifically Catholic here", which is as good as saying, "You'd be as well off going elsewhere." This speaks of Catholicism as a faith among faiths, all of them equally valid paths to the divine. Here the doctrine of the Theosophists has won the day, the idea that all the world religions represent man's attempt to encounter the one, great universal spirit that underlies everything. The status of Catholicism as the revealed religion of the one, true God is therefore denied.

—The typical Relativist church focuses on the gathering of the "People of God". The new church building is intended as a place for the individual to encounter "God through the worshipping community". The message here is that the church building has no meaning unless liturgical celebrations are taking place within it. It is designed, first and foremost, for the worship of the assembly, and not to reflect the mystery of the Church, which is the communion of God and mankind through Christ's sacrifice, Resurrection, and ascension. The principle of the church as a sacramental building visibly representing the Church, the Kingdom of God mysteriously present, has been dropped, thereby denying the transcendent vision and insisting only on the significance of the here and now. Also ignored is the company of Heaven, the angels, the communion of saints, the dead, and anyone else who is simply not present.

— And the layout of the typical Relativist church promotes activity, the aim being the mistranslated "active participation" of the people. (*Participatio actuosa* means "actual participation".) The concept of a "creative liturgy" is consistently promoted, which implies that the liturgy is evolving and constantly being shaped and made better, although such a state can never be achieved, because who is to decide what is better? This allows the tastes and preferences of the congregation to dominate and undermines the concept of the liturgy as a gift from God to the whole Church. It also undermines the value of continuity with the traditions of the past, which by definition must be inferior to the experiments of today. The very look of the new church implies impermanence. Its internal spaces are open plan so as not to impede the free expression of the "people of God" and to allow for maximum flexibility. Its furnishings are flimsy and unsubstantial—the lectern will most likely be portable and free-standing; the chairs can be stacked and moved aside; the altar resembles a table, which may be pushed against a wall so that a concert can be held. As in many ideas of the modern age, the search for faith is valued over the expression and deepening of faith. Consequently, novelties and innovations abound. Restlessness becomes a key feature of worship in the new church.

The documents, mentioned above, and the countless church buildings designed according to their principles, have as their central idea the concept of "universal" space, space that is undifferentiated and nonhierarchical. The link between the architecture of built space in any age and the architecture of the model of the universe of that age has been mentioned in Chapter I above. Modernist architecture, with its ideas about free-flowing, unbounded space, reflects the universal model of its time. But is it appropriate that the church building should also do this, given that the Relativist universe has been emptied of the divine and therefore of all meaning? The Church does not have to adopt an architectural style just because it happens to be current, a style embodying a universal model that is bound to pass as did those preceding it.

Below are some examples of Relativist church buildings. This is an entirely random sample and does not suggest that the churches described here are any worse than countless other churches. Unfortunately there are far too many like them.

* * *

I. Reordered Churches

Saint Joseph's, Bunhill Row, London, England

As much of a disaster as the design and construction of Relativist church buildings from scratch has been the re-ordering of existing churches. Comparable with the stripping of the altars that took place during the Protestant Reformation, this new "Modernist Reformation" has overseen the denuding of Catholic churches across the world.

The prospect of a much-loved church being reordered has been known to strike fear into hearts, just as the designation "scheduled for redevelopment" used to cast shadows over entire neighborhoods as city planners and architects set about replacing them with vast networks of concrete blocks and towers. At first, both church reorderings and neighborhood redevelopments were hailed as necessary steps toward a bright, new future, and the unsuspecting public accepted the arguments of the modernizers, that is, until they had to live with the results. Then the arguments started, the protests began, and the adverse publicity grew to such a volume that the secular planners and architects, at least, were forced to abandon their visions and create proper city environments again.

In the Church, however, the arguments have only just begun, which is not surprising since the Church, by attempting to be both in the world *and* of the world, ends up being behind the world—by about thirty years. And although there have been some recent cases of the re-reordering of churches, in other words the restoration of what was once deemed superfluous and removed, the reorderings continue, and Saint Joseph's, Bunhill Row, has seen more than its fair share of them.

The first reordering took place in the 1970s and resulted in the bare, scooped-out look so common at the time. For the next twenty years the church was threatened with closure, and a consequent lack of maintenance resulted in a severely neglected interior and entrance. Then, with its future secure and a new parish priest, a program of renovation work was begun in 1991 and completed two years later.

As part of the work, which included structural repairs, the church interior was completely redesigned in a

1
Saint Joseph's, Bunhill Row, London, England.
1922 altar.

2
Saint Joseph's, Bunhill Row, London, England.
Altar after 1970s reordering.

"Florentine, Renaissance style", explained architect Anthony
Delarue,

which happily accommodated the fine Italianate windows, the only surviving original feature from the old
Saint Mary Moorfields, the former proto-cathedral.

In order to define the sanctuary, which architecturally
was merely an extension of the nave, the new altar was
raised an additional step, a curtained canopy was placed
above it and the tabernacle was returned to the centre,
the only liturgically and symbolically satisfactory arrangement in such a narrow area. The sanctuary walls were
painted in "faux-marble" and statues of the Sacred Heart
and Our Lady placed at the entrance to the nave in front

of new pilasters which emphasised the distinct and sacred nature of this area of the church.

Statues which previously had been lined up in a row at the back were restored and rehoused in new shrines, the black marble baptismal font was restored and relocated, and a new confessional in the traditional "closed" arrangement with a grill was constructed to replace the confessional removed during the 1970's re-ordering. Finally, the entrance was renovated by constructing a new classical arch with iron gates and setting a statue of St Joseph above the door.[9]

In the years that followed, parish life began to flourish again as devotions were fostered and grew, including the Rosary, the Forty Hours devotion, and Corpus Christi processions. There were catechism classes, traditional sacred music and chant during the Mass, and local people who had lapsed from the Church years ago were beginning to come back.

Then a new priest came to the parish who is reported as saying, "The trouble with the Saint Joseph's parishioners is that they are too devotional." This was not long after cutting down the altar canopy one evening with a bread knife and leaving the pieces, together with the knife, on the altar. The story is that the ladies who came the following morning to help prepare the church for the day assumed that vandals had broken into the church during the night and were about to telephone the police when the new priest appeared and explained that he had done it.

Next to be removed from the sanctuary were the altar rails, and then the statues of our Lady and the Sacred Heart. The Friday Rosary was canceled, the organist who had introduced

---

[9] From an interview conducted by the Author.

3
Saint Joseph's, Bunhill Row, London, England.
Altar and sanctuary after 1990s restoration.

sacred music to the Mass was dismissed, and the pews were rearranged to face the altar diagonally so as not to appear too formal, the aim being to introduce a "creative liturgy" to Saint Joseph's. The Corpus Christi procession that had recently been reinstated in the parish was dropped, a number of statues were removed from their new shrines and stored in a cupboard, and the Christmas crib was disposed of as rubbish. Then a new and unadorned, almost square, wooden altar was introduced, the "faux marble" was painted over, and new, minimalist sanctuary furniture was added.

"I used to think that once a reordered church had been restored and its devotional and parish life was flourishing, that the restoration couldn't be reversed", said Anthony

4
Saint Joseph's, Bunhill Row, London, England.
Altar following reordering in 2002–2003.

Delarue. "It seems I was wrong." [10] Over recent years, Saint Joseph's has been reordered, re-reordered, and then reordered again. The effect this has had on the parishioners depends on who is asked. Some claim a renewed vision of parish life. Others now attend Mass in another parish.

Cathedral of Saint John the Evangelist, Milwaukee, U.S.A.

Milwaukee's Archbishop Rembert Weakland had plans to reorder Saint John's that included the dismantling of an ornate,

[10] Ibid.

forty-foot-high dome baldachino, which, in a letter to priests, deacons, and parish administrators in the Archdiocese of Milwaukee, July 5, 2001, he claimed, had "no artistic or historic value". His plans also involved removing the high altar and placing a much smaller altar in the center of the nave, replacing pews with chairs for more flexible seating and arranging them around the new altar, moving the tabernacle to a side chapel, formerly the baptistry, converting the baptismal font into a shallow pool with running water, and relocating the choir in the apse. The new and much smaller altar was to rest on columns recycled from side altars, and the new bishop's chair was to be made from marble taken from the communion rail that had been removed in 1976.

As a result of a protest campaign by the local laity, the Vatican's Congregation for Divine Worship sent a letter to Archbishop Weakland demanding that he explain the need for the proposed changes. The CDW then wrote a letter to local protesters that included the following: "Having received further information about the project from Archbishop Rembert Weakland which nonetheless left doubts that the project would conform to canonical and liturgical norms, we moved to suspend the work of renovation until these doubts may be clarified."[11]

Undeterred, the Archbishop ordered the work to go ahead anyway and wrote to every priest in the diocese accusing a "small group in Rome, in Milwaukee and in the United States" of trying to humiliate him before he retired. The work is estimated to have cost $4.5 million, and a rededication ceremony for the new Saint John's took place in 2002. The Vatican accepted Archbishop Weakland's offer to resign at seventy-five, and he has since moved to

---

[11] *The Catholic Herald* (London: Herald House, June 8, 2001).

5
Cathedral of Saint John the Evangelist, Milwaukee, U.S.A.
The baldachino before reordering.

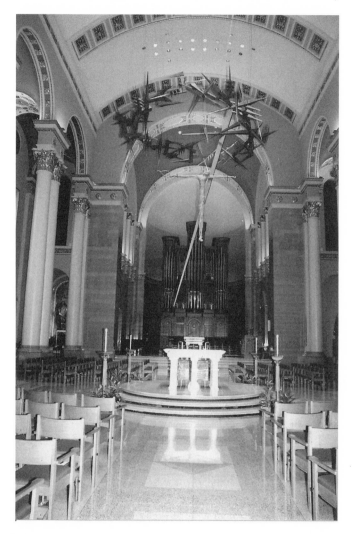

6
Cathedral of Saint John the Evangelist, Milwaukee, U.S.A.
The new altar in 2002 following reordering.

a small cottage on the grounds of a monastery to seek "prayers and healing".[12]

2. Concrete Brutalism

Cathedral Church of Saints Peter and Paul, Bristol, England

Among the hallmarks of the "New Brutalist" architecture of the 1950s and 1960s were the shuttering marks deliberately left in concrete walls and ceilings to show just how unfussy the aesthetic really was. To build using concrete poured onsite, as opposed to concrete panels precast in a factory, molds first have to be assembled using timber planks, or shuttering, which leave their imprint on the surface of the concrete as it sets. These "shuttering marks" became a symbol of the unadorned Brutalist style, as did vast areas of concrete, unadorned exteriors, and informal groupings of buildings that meander across a site as topography dictates, rather than following any imposed organizational plane.

Clifton Cathedral, as the cathedral church is known locally, was designed by the Percy Thomas Partnership, and seems to have been designed with meandering in mind. Inside, an area called the narthex merges into another area called the baptistry, which merges into the nave, which is barely distinguishable from the sanctuary. And somewhere there is a Blessed Sacrament chapel, if you can find it. So downplayed is its presence that you might easily meander past it several times without noticing. During my visit on a Saturday afternoon, no one else was to be seen, and the empty space

[12] Ibid.

7
Cathedral Church of Saints Peter and Paul, (Clifton Cathedral), Bristol,
England, 1973.
Architects—The Percy Thomas Partnership.
Interior.

seemed little more than—well, empty space—which had
a decidedly depressing effect after no time at all. The
approaches to the cathedral are typically devoid of symbolism, and inside there is concrete everywhere, with a splash
of abstractly patterned stained glass here and there.

The 1973 brochure describing the design and construction of Clifton Cathedral, Bristol, agrees with E. A. Sovik
that churches are not really necessary. It states that "Most
informed Christians are well aware that the buildings we
call churches are not strictly essential for Christianity. It

is the Christian himself who is the temple of the living God." [13]

The suggestion here is that only *uninformed* Christians believe that churches are essential for Christianity, and that it is up to the enlightened and the educated to point out the error of this belief. Armed with a partial interpretation of *Sacrosanctum Concilium* and all the usual buzz words, the brochure makes it clear that a church building is no longer to be considered a sacred place where Christ is made truly present through the sacrifice of the Mass, the reenactment of His sacrifice on Calvary. Instead, churches have become "assembly" places where the "People of God" are invited to have an "active role" and to "gather round the altar".

The hewn, Portland stone altar is square to facilitate con-celebration and to express participation by all the people in the Mass. According to the cathedral brochure, the silver chalice represents the offerings of both "man's life and work" and "the sacrifice of Christ". So Christ gets a mention at last, although His sacrifice is somehow secondary to the offering of man's life and work.

The cathedral was commissioned in 1965, as the liturgical revolution was gaining momentum. In 1970 the foundation stone was laid, and work was completed three years later.

Basilica of Our Lady of Guadalupe, Mexico City

Constructed on the site of the sixteenth-century basilica, which had to be demolished due to structural problems, the new basilica was designed by Pedro Ramírez Vásquez and completed in 1976. Inside, the floor plan is circular,

---

[13] Brochure of Cathedral Church of SS. Peter and Paul (Bristol: Clifton Cathedral House, 1973).

8
Basilica of Our Lady of Guadalupe, Mexico City, 1976.
Architect—Pedro Ramírez Vásquez.
Exterior.

and the choir is located between the altar and the faithful
to indicate, apparently, that the choir "is part of the group
of the faithful".[14] The basilica boasts an empty crucifix to
symbolize Christ's Resurrection (despite the fact that Christ
rose from the tomb and not the Cross) and has seven front
doors to represent the seven gates of the celestial Jerusalem.

That is what the publicity says anyway, as if all it takes to
invoke the celestial Jerusalem is to incorporate seven of something, doors or windows or even drainage ducts, into a featureless concrete drum of a building, which, quite unlike
the celestial Jerusalem, should be demolished at once.

[14] www.sancta.org.

9
Basilica of Our Lady of Guadalupe, Mexico City, 1976.
Architect—Pedro Ramírez Vásquez.
Interior.

3. Not Really Churches

Our Lady of the Angels Cathedral, Los Angeles, U.S.A.

The cathedral could be an office building, a shopping mall, or a multiscreen cinema complex. It has the look of a building that does not want to admit that it is a church. Its promoters praise it ecstatically and have produced an expensive and glossy brochure full of high-quality photographs of a building that is barely distinguishable from its neighbors.[15] Inside, the look is minimal, with the vast areas of

---

[15] Michael Downey, *The Cathedral: At the Heart of Los Angeles*, 2nd ed. (Collegeville, Minn.: Liturgical Press, 2003).

bare concrete, wood, and clear glass considered appropriate for the contemporary worship space.

In forty-two pages there is only one mention in the brochure of the Mass, which is listed as one of the many "activities" taking place in the cathedral and that are also deemed central to the faith, like "hosting banquets" and "supporting the oppressed". This is a cathedral "for people" according to the brochure, a building "where the human heart and its deepest longings can find rest ... a setting for the most precious of jewels—God's people ... a place for

10
Our Lady of the Angels Cathedral, Los Angeles, 2002.
Architect—Raphael Moneo.
Exterior.

11
Our Lady of the Angels Cathedral, Los Angeles, 2002.
Architect—Raphael Moneo.
Interior.

everything that ennobles the human spirit: fine art, music, folk craft, worship and more". At least worship is included in the list, although the Blessed Sacrament is not.

In *Ugly As Sin: Why They Changed Our Churches from Sacred Places to Meeting Spaces—and How We Can Change Them Back Again*, Michael Rose writes of Our Lady of the Angels:

> The new Cathedral ... has been described by critics in L.A. as a "yellow armadillo." Christian iconography on the façades is minimal, and the symbolism that is used is said to be more "inclusive" and "universally appealing" than specifically Catholic. One Archdiocese of Los Angeles official explained that "you don't need St. Peter and St. Paul over the entrance." Rather, he admitted, the new Our Lady of the Angels cathedral "avoids assigning meaning," although in the same breath he begrudgingly conceded that the L.A. Cathedral "obviously will have a certain amount of rhetoric brought into it because it has a certain use.". . . The faceless façade is appropriate for the modern non-church centrum. It's an accurate prelude to the worship space within.[16]

The Cathedral of Our Lady of the Angels was designed by Raphael Moneo and completed in 2002.

Padre Pio Pilgrimage Church, Puglia, Italy

Completed in 2004, the Padre Pio Pilgrimage Church was designed by the Renzo Piano Building Workshop. Renzo Piano, former partner of the architect Richard Rogers who designed the Pompidou Centre in Paris, has stated that his

---

[16] Michael S. Rose, *Ugly As Sin: Why They Changed Our Churches from Sacred Places to Meeting Spaces—and How We Can Change Them Back Again* (Manchester, N.H.: Sophia Institute Press, 2001), 169. Copyright 2001 Michael S. Rose.

12
Padre Pio Pilgrimage Church, Puglia, Italy, 2004.
Architects—The Renzo Piano Building Workshop.

aim was "to create the modern equivalent of a gothic cathedral but to make the arches fly within the space".[17] Again the circular, or semicircular plan is employed to enable people to gather round the altar, which makes this design entirely *unlike* any church that would have been built in the Middle Ages. Renzo Piano is reported not to like the monumentality of Saint Peter's in Rome. Instead he prefers "to create an open church" which "has not been given a monumental façade, but simply a glass front".

In order that the Padre Pio Pilgimage Church should actually resemble a church, stone was chosen as a construction material because of "an instinctive memory of the church built of stone". While this very minor concession at least acknowledges that people's customary conceptions might have some significance, if this most contemporary church building is noted for anything, it will be for its technical achievements. In order that its structure might achieve a span of over 54 yards (over 50 meters), each differently sized and shaped segment of stone had to be specially cut with

[17] *Church Building Magazine*, no. 71 (September/October 2001).

the aid of computerized cutting machines. The arches are secured by internal cables, which are not precompressed but which become compressed in the event of an earthquake.

However, despite the ingenious use of a traditional material, the design is the "modern equivalent of a gothic cathedral" in name only. Only a glance at the drawings reveals its overwhelming horizontality, which is so typical of today's church buildings. All the technical effort has gone into enveloping a horizontal space, whereas the medieval architects and stonemasons were masters of the vertical, their aim being the creation of spaces that soared upward, thereby lifting the heart and the mind to God. Despite the obvious expertise that has gone into this building, the design of Padre Pio Church signifies one thing: a turning away from a universe that, in the modern mind, has been emptied of God.

Chapel of Reconciliation, Walsingham, England

Opened in 1981, the Chapel of Reconciliation has the appearance of a barn. Perhaps the aim was to produce a building that would go unnoticed in its rural setting, being adjacent to the Slipper Chapel where medieval pilgrims would leave their shoes and walk barefoot to the shrine in the village of Walsingham a mile away. This might have been acceptable, if the intention had been to surprise today's pilgrims with the treat of a full-fledged church interior. But it clearly was not the intention, since the interior is as dreadful as could be.

Today's pilgrim has to find the entrance doors first, which are so understated they could almost be invisible, then pass through a mean little lobby to enter the body of the church. Directly opposite this entrance is another set of entrance

13
Chapel of Reconciliation, Walsingham, England, 1981.
Exterior.

doors, which means that the pilgrim has to pivot on the
spot in order to approach what is described as the sanctuary. And of course the seating is arranged so that the people can "gather round the altar", and there is carpet on the
floor to make people feel at home, although no one has a
home that looks like this.

The big feature of the Chapel of Reconciliation is the par-
tition doors allowing the "sanctuary" to be opened to the exterior during summer months when pilgrim numbers reach their
peak, thereby allowing Mass to be heard by those outside. And
you may as well be outside as in the chapel, so featureless is

14
Chapel of Reconciliation, Walsingham, England, 1981.
Interior.

its interior. One parishioner told me, "We had to pray for five years to get a tabernacle in here. That's what we got, but at least it's something. Before they used to reserve the Blessed Sacrament in a cupboard in the sacristy."

The prayed-for tabernacle seems to be made out of plastic and sits on the floor somewhere to the side. There are no statues, you cannot light a candle, the overhead steel beams are exposed, and there is bare brickwork everywhere. All in all, it is about as drab a church building as can be found anywhere and a terrible indictment of the liturgical revolution that spawned it.

4. The White Box

Chiesa Dio Padre Misericordioso, Jubilee Church, Rome

The current fashion for the all-white display space has produced some startling results, such as New York's renovated Museum of Modern Art and London's Tate Modern gallery. The "white box" might have become the obligatory style of any "happening" art gallery, but the question here is whether or not this style is appropriate for the church building.

Breda Ennis, professor of fine arts at Rome's American University, certainly has her doubts. In an article for *Sacred Architecture*, on the Jubilee Church in Rome's outskirts, which was completed in 2000 and designed by Richard Meier, she writes:

> Pope John Paul II suggested that art can serve as "a kind of bridge to religious experience". I agree wholeheartedly. But I doubt very much if the Meier Church succeeds in being that kind of bridge. After several visits to "Dio Padre Misericordioso", my impression is that, if the building can be described in any sense as "a bridge", it is a bridge which serves simply to lift us up, or bring us into one of the zones of the (by now) familiar modernist enterprise.[18]

Six international architects were invited to present their ideas for the Jubilee Church, and it was agreed by the commission responsible for choosing the final design that the architect need not be a Christian believer. The design, which is reminiscent of the Sydney Opera House, is certainly capable of attracting the eye, with its glaring whiteness, curved "sail" walls, and large areas of plain glass. But as with many

---

[18] Breda Ennis, "A Vacuum in the Spirit: The Design of the Jubilee Church in Rome", *Sacred Architecture*, vol. 9 (Fall/Winter 2004).

15
Chiesa Dio Padre Misericordioso, Jubilee Church, Rome, 2000.
Architect—Richard Meier and Partners.
Exterior.

Modernist projects, the attempt to create a design that can startle has raised all manner of construction questions, not to mention the budget, which originally was intended to be $5 million, but eventually reached $25 million.

The curved walls presented technical problems requiring over two hundred precast blocks, each weighing twelve tons, to be placed in position by a specially constructed, moving crane that took three months to assemble and could not be used if wind speeds reached more than 25 miles (40 kilometers) per hour, which they frequently did. Special training was required to use the crane, and the first curved wall took seven months to construct, the second took five months, and the third took six months.

16
Chiesa Dio Padre Misericordioso, Jubilee Church, Rome, 2000.
Architect—Richard Meier and Partners.
Interior.

Breda Ennis describes her first visit to the Jubilee Church. "There in front of me I saw a mass of snow-white walls, both curved and straight, held together by glass and surrounded by a pale paved area and a low wall.... Looking though the glass facade, the eye comes to rest on the wall which divides the nave from the atrium or narthex, and you think that this cannot be the entrance because you do not immediately see the inner door."

Once inside, she describes how the "stark interiors and raw geometry" of the building coupled with the lack of any distinct "change of space" between the nave and the sanctuary, contrast sharply with the traditional Roman churches to which she is accustomed. This is hardly surprising, since everything about this Modernist church building project contrasts sharply with tradition.

The "white box" represents the very latest in contemporary church design. Its enthusiasts talk about the purity of their interiors and of how they are flooded with white light from so much uncolored, hard-to-keep clean glazing, as if being dazzled by white light represents the height of spiritual experience. But white light is not pure at all, since it is made up of all the colors of the spectrum and being blinded by it is yet another reason for turning away from the transcendent and looking inward.

* * *

In *Catholic Thought Since the Enlightenment*, Aidan Nichols, O.P., writes:

the Modernists gave the impression that doctrine was simply a vehicle for the response of a given age to the divine. A doctrine well suited to the time-spirit of one generation

might be gawkily out of place in another. Instead of
saying that there is a historical dimension to the explic-
itation of doctrine, evolution becomes everything. And
... in revelation the Modernists appeared to be claiming that the orientation of the human spirit to tran-
scendence was the entire explanation of the Christian
religion. Scriptures, sacraments, dogmas, Church insti-
tutions become so many symbolic forms thrown up by
the movement of the human spirit toward God in history. Instead of saying that the intrinsic ordination of
humankind to God is a necessary complement to the
external signs and teachings of divine revelation, interior-
ity becomes everything.[19]

The development and spread of Modernist ideas did not
go unchallenged in the Church. Throughout the nineteenth century, the proponents of Neoscholasticism attempted
to counteract them, and in 1879 Pope Leo XIII ordered
the teaching of Thomist philosophy in schools and seminar-
ies.[20] This was not the first time that a pope would resist
the advance of contemporary ideas into theology, ideas chal-
lenging many of the tenets of the traditional system. The
1907 Encyclical Letter of Pope Pius X, *Pascendi Dominici
Gregis* (*On the Doctrine of the Modernists*), described the Modernist belief in "vital immanence", which denies external
revelation and instead looks for an explanation of religion
in the life of man. Proceeding from this belief is the principle of "religious immanence", which the Modernists

[19] Aidan Nichols, O.P., *Catholic Thought Since the Enlightenment: A Survey*
(Leominster, Eng.: Gracewing Publishing, 1998), 84.
[20] Pope Leo XIII, Encyclical Letter, *Aeterni Patris: On the Establishment of
Christian Philosophy in the Tradition of St Thomas Aquinas, the Angelic Doctor, in
Our Catholic Schools* (1879; reprint Boston: Pauline Books and Media, n.d.).

describe as a movement of the heart, a movement called a "sense". This the Modernists claim to be the origin of religion, according to the encyclical.[21]

Religious faith therefore becomes the result of God revealing himself to the individual through an interior religious "sense", and this "experience" of God makes the individual a believer. The Modernists then assert that the interior religious sense is also the source of *revelation*, and that, as a result, consciousness and revelation are synonymous and equally valid. And from this assertion it follows that Catholicism is a development of the interior religious sense of Man and that dogmas are both "symbols" of certain aspects of the religious sense and its "instruments", in that they help the individual understand the religious sense. But in no way can they be considered fixed. Instead they are capable of being adapted to the needs of the age and the individual.

As the encyclical points out,

> Therefore, as God is the object of religion, we must conclude that faith, which is the basis and foundation of all religion, must consist in a certain interior sense, originating in a need of the divine. This need of the divine, which is experienced only in special and favourable circumstances, cannot of itself appertain to the domain of consciousness, but is first latent beneath consciousness, or, to borrow a term from modern philosophy, in the *subconsciousness*, where also its root lies hidden and undetected.[22]

---

[21] Pope Pius X, Encyclical Letter, *Pascendi Dominici Gregis: On the Doctrine of the Modernists* (September 8, 1907; reprint Boston: Pauline Books and Media, n.d.).

[22] Ibid., par. 7.

The encyclical also observes that

> here it is well to note at once that, given this doctrine of *experience* united with that of *symbolism*, every religion, even that of paganism, must be held to be true. What is to prevent such experiences from being found in any religion? In fact, that they are so is maintained by not a few. On what grounds can Modernists deny the truth of an experience affirmed by a follower of Islam? Will they claim a monopoly of true experiences for Catholics alone? Indeed, Modernists do not deny, but actually maintain, some confusedly, others frankly, that all religions are true.[23]

Here we have the basis of a new way of looking at things. A group of individuals, at a particular moment in time and history, were moved by their interior religious sense to formulate a set of beliefs and dogmas expressing their ideas about God, and this set of beliefs and dogmas became Catholicism. Meanwhile other groups of individuals, at different moments in time and history, were being moved by their interior religious sense to formulate sets of beliefs and dogmas to express *their* ideas about God, who had also revealed Himself to *them* in the depths of their souls. These sets of beliefs and dogmas became Buddhism and Hinduism, for example.

In a similar vein, the individuals who had lived in Palestine under the occupation of the Roman Empire happened to translate their experience of God revealing Himself to their inner religious sense in a manner that was practical and applicable to their time and circumstances. But modern man lives under different circumstances and is bound to interpret differently the experience of God revealing

---

[23] Ibid., par. 14.

Himself to *his* inner religious sense. Accordingly, revelation must be subject to different interpretations, and even be made entirely new, as the needs of the times change. And once the theory of evolution is brought into the picture, along with the notion that twentieth-century man is more developed than first-century man, the necessity for the continual revision of dogma becomes established, based on the following propositions:

— that truth is relative to a given culture or period in history. What was true and relevant during the Middle Ages or the Baroque period is not necessarily true or relevant today;

— that God makes Himself present within the individual as does the desire for God. Revelation is therefore the result of both God's self-communication to Man and Man's awakening to God. Because God makes Himself present within the individual and the Church is a community of believers, not an institution or system, it is the worshipping community that is the visible sign of God's presence; and

— that dogma and tradition are expressions of human understanding of the Divine at a particular time and place and are therefore bound to change.

Less than two decades before the Second Vatican Council, the Encyclical Letter of Pope Pius XII, *Humani Generis* (*Some False Opinions Which Threaten to Undermine Catholic Doctrine*),[24] makes a number of relevant points:

---

[24] Pope Pius XII, Encyclical Letter, *Humani Generis: Some False Opinions which Threaten to Undermine Catholic Doctrine* (August 12, 1950; Boston: Pauline Books and Media, n.d.).

In theology some want to reduce to a minimum the
meaning of dogmas.... They cherish the hope that when
dogma is stripped of the elements which they hold to
be extrinsic to divine revelation, it will compare ad-
vantageously with the dogmatic opinions of those who
are separated from the unity of the Church and that in
this way they will gradually arrive at a mutual assimi-
lation of Catholic dogma with the tenets of the dissi-
dents. (par. 14)

Moreover they assert that when Catholic doctrine has
been reduced to this condition, a way will be found to
satisfy modern needs, that will permit of dogma being
expressed by the concepts of modern philosophy, whether
of immanentism or idealism or existentialism or any other
system.... They add that the history of dogmas consists
in the reporting of the various forms in which revealed
truth has been clothed, forms that have succeeded one
another in accordance with the different teachings and
opinions that have arisen over the courses of the centuries. (par. 15)

It is evident from what We have already said, that
such tentatives not only lead to what they call dogmatic relativism, but that they actually contain it. (par.
16) Hence to neglect, or to reject, or to devalue so
many and such great resources which have been conceived, expressed and perfected so often by the age-old
work of men endowed with no common talent and
holiness, working under the vigilant supervision of the
holy magisterium and with the light and leadership of
the Holy Ghost in order to state the truths of the faith
ever more accurately, to do this so that these things
may be replaced by conjectural notions and by some
formless and unstable tenets of a new philosophy, tenets
which, like the flowers of the field, are in existence
today and die tomorrow; this is supreme imprudence

and something that would make dogmas itself a reed shaken by the wind. (par. 17)

It is well worth noting the words of Monsignor Klaus Gamber, who writes in *The Reform of the Roman Liturgy: Its Problems and Background*:

Never before in history have so many churches been built as during the years immediately following the Second World War. The majority of them were utilitarian structures not designed to be works of art, yet they often cost millions to build. From a technical standpoint, they are well equipped: they have good acoustics and superb air conditioning; they are well lit and can be easily heated. The altar can be seen from all directions.

Still, they are not houses of God in the true sense: they are not a sanctuary, they are not a temple of the Lord that we can visit to adore God and ask for His grace and assistance. They are meeting facilities, places nobody wants to visit at any time other than when services are being conducted. They are designed like "apartment silos" or "people garages", as we refer to the housing complexes in our modern suburbs—church buildings which in colloquial terms are "soul silos" or "Pater noster garages".

In contrast, the pilgrimage church at Ronchamp has been used as a model for all those church buildings designed and built specifically as works of art. In building this church, the well-known architect Le Corbusier, a professed agnostic, has created a true architectural work of art. *Yet, in the end, it did not turn out to be a church.* At best it is a place to pray, to meditate. But the church at Ronchamp has become a model and meeting place for subjectivist architects. This development in the design of church buildings could only come about because of a growing conviction that there are no such things as "sacred spaces" that are (or should be) different from the profane world.

The new buildings are a symbol of our time, even an indication of the dissolution of traditional norms and standards and a representation of the chaotic nature of the world in which we live.[25]

Not every church architect is conscious of all this, naturally. Some are practicing Catholics who believe they are following the directives of the Church, having been influenced by the "spirit of Vatican II" and not having read the actual Council documents themselves. They are attracted by the ideas of unity and active participation without realizing their efforts end up detracting from God. Many are not aware of the theosophical roots of modern styles and principles of art and architecture. And some do try to incorporate beauty into their designs, not subscribing to the barren look or lack of color. Their reason for downsizing imagery is to draw attention to the Mass itself, considering a plethora of statues as distracting.

Unfortunately, such reasoning forgets that as fallen creatures, we will become distracted even if there is nothing else to look at. In fact, the more bland the room, the easier it will be for us either to look at other people or to fall into a daydream. One of the reasons for having statues and stained glass windows, aside from their beauty, is so that when our eyes wander, they fall upon a saint or a Bible story, something that will bring our minds back to God. They also are helpful to children, who, with their shorter attention spans, find it even harder to focus on the Mass;

[25] Klaus Gamber, *The Reform of the Roman Liturgy: Its Problems and Background* (San Juan Capistrano, Calif.: Una Voce Press, 1993), 122.

for those children too young to read, images also provide a catechism in pictures.

There is an interesting parallel between the reordering of school classrooms and the reordering of churches, which began at around the same time. The ideas behind both came to a head in the 1960s and began to be put in place a decade later.

Gone was the formality and hierarchy of the traditional way. Pupils no longer sat at desks in rows facing the front. Instead they gathered in groups around tables. Teachers were no longer the imparters of knowledge. Instead they became facilitators, their new role being to help the student (not pupil) take an active role in the educational process. Classrooms became "activity zones", and the walls between them were dismantled. Students moved from history zone, to art zone, to language zone on their journeys of discovery. Education became child-centered, just as the liturgy became people-centered.

The new catechetics stressed that revelation is no longer a body of truth revealed by Christ to be taught by His Church to each succeeding generation. Instead revelation came to be described as "God speaking to you in your heart". Religious education became the discovery of the truth within, a process of experiencing and finding out. According to the new ideas, traditional formulas and dogmas were redundant, and the prayers of old were no longer appropriate. After all, why learn an ancient prayer when you can make up a new one?

The teaching of spelling and grammar were deemed to stifle the creativity and free expression of the child and were dropped. The three R's—reading, writing, and arithmetic— were considered far too oppressive for the modern child, with the result that a generation of schoolchildren were not taught how to read, write, or add. Eventually the government was forced to acknowledge that modern education had produced the least literate graduates in Europe and to urge a return to more traditional teaching methods. This, of course, is being resisted by the 1960s gurus of the new educational methods.

The Early Church

"According to St. Basil and other Church Fathers, the custom of turning towards the east when praying goes back to apostolic times." So writes Titus Burckhardt in *Chartres and the Birth of the Cathedral.* He goes on: "The early Christians saw in the sun, which on Easter morning rises precisely in the east, the natural image of the Saviour who had risen from death to life. *The house of the believers*, according to what is written in the approximately 400 Apostolic Constitutions, *is long in shape like a ship (nave) and directed towards the east.* The later liturgists added that the place of the equinox should be used as an orientation guide." [1]

In *The Modern Rite: Collected Essays on the Reform of the Liturgy* Klaus Gamber describes typical dining arrangements in Mediterranean cultures at the time of Christ, in order to answer any notion that the celebration of Mass facing the people reflects the seating arrangements at the Last Supper.[2] With the postconciliar emphasis on the Mass as a communal meal, the argument goes, it is fitting that priest and people should gather round the altar just as Christ and the Apostles would have gathered round the table.

---

[1] Titus Burckhardt, *Chartres and the Birth of the Cathedral* (Ipswich, U.K.: Golgonooza Press, 1995), 15.

[2] Klaus Gamber, *The Modern Rite: Collected Essays on the Reform of the Liturgy*, trans. Scott M. P. Reid (Farnborough, Eng.: Saint Michael's Abbey Press, 2002), 26.

But in fact it was customary at the time for meals and banquets to be held around semicircular or crescent-shaped tables, with all the guests sitting on the outside and the food being served from the inside. In other words, the guests all sat on one side of the table and were served from the other side. According to this seating arrangement, at the Last Supper, Christ and the Apostles would have faced the same direction, the direction from where the food was being served.

This then is the arrangement that formed the basis of the earliest Christian worship. Tables were laid out, and the people sat around three sides facing the east, where the host was consecrated. Later the form was adapted, and the people stood before a single altar, again orientated toward the east. Thus the form of the earliest churches was orientated toward a single symbolic direction, and priest and people together faced the same way.

Steven Schloeder also writes of this eastward orientation in *Architecture in Communion: Implementing the Second Vatican Council through Liturgy and Architecture*:

> In the early Syrian churches, there seems to have been great room for flexibility in placing the altar. While it perhaps most frequently stood against the rear wall of the apse, it could also be placed on the chord of the apse, in the nave at the chancel steps, or even in the middle of the nave. Regardless of the position of the altar, the Eucharist was always celebrated towards the east, by both priest and people, as part of the cosmic liturgy. Interestingly, in the early Egyptian churches where the priest was "facing the people", the people were called to "Turn to the east!" at the eucharistic prayer. They were expected to turn their backs to the altar for the entire canon of the Mass, including during the

Consecration, which shows the immense value given to liturgical orientation.[3]

When the emperor Constantine legalized Christianity in the fourth century, church building began in earnest. Again there is no evidence of the form of the community gathering currently being promoted. (The first Christians may have met in one another's houses because they had nowhere else to go.) While the layout of the early Christian churches was based on the form of the Roman basilica, their orientation was derived from the Temple in Jerusalem, where the main doors were in the east and the altar in the west.

The layout of the Constantinian basilicas can sometimes give the impression that Mass facing the people was the practice at the time. But this is a misreading of the evidence. In the old Saint Peter's, which was rebuilt in the sixteenth century, the altar was in the west and faced the main doors in the east. This is also the arrangement in the new Saint Peter's. The traditional custom, however, was for the people to stand not in the nave facing the altar, which was veiled, but at the sides, also facing the east. Again this arrangement emphasized the turning of both priest and people together toward the east.

According to Steven Schloeder, with the growth of the monasteries and the subsequent multiplication of Masses, side altars began to be orientated toward the east. The position of the priest at the side altar was such that priest and people faced the same way, and this was gradually adopted for high altars as well. Then, by the tenth century, the predominant position was of the priest facing an altar against the east wall.

---

[3] Steven Schloeder, *Architecture in Communion: Implementing the Second Vatican Council through Liturgy and Architecture* (San Francisco: Ignatius Press, 1998), 71.

Anyone who has visited the catacombs outside Rome will have noticed the wall-facing altars, built over the tombs of martyrs, which again demonstrate the common orientation of priest and people during Mass. The evidence is that orientation was considered to be of great significance in the early Church.

In *The Spirit of the Liturgy* Cardinal Ratzinger writes of the rationale of facing the east: "Praying toward the east means going to meet the coming Christ. The liturgy, turned towards the east, effects entry, so to speak, into the procession of history toward the future, the New Heaven and the New Earth, which we encounter in Christ. . . ." But, finally, "this turning toward the east also signifies that cosmos and saving history belong together. The cosmos is praying with us. It, too, is waiting for redemption. It is precisely this cosmic dimension that is essential to Christian liturgy." [4]

An understanding of the prevailing universal model at the time of the early Church may also give insight into the significance of the cosmic dimension to Christians in the earliest centuries, who lived in a very different universe to the modern version. The verticality of the universe known by the early Church could not have produced inward-looking church buildings where people "gather round the altar", church buildings inspired by the Relativist universe of today. A vertical universal model does not call people to gather round, but to reach out and move forward. The actions of gathering round and moving forward are mutually exclusive.

This was a universe with a clear distinction between "nature", which was composed of the four elements—air,

[4] Joseph Cardinal Ratzinger, *The Spirit of the Liturgy* (San Francisco: Ignatius Press, 2000), 69.

fire, earth, and water—and "sky", which was of an entirely different substance—ether. The astronomer Ptolemy of Alexandria, who died around A.D. 140, first mapped out the planetary orbits showing a universe of concentric spheres, like those Russian dolls that keep opening to reveal yet another smaller doll inside. According to his model, first in orbit around the earth was the moon, then Mercury, Venus, Mars, the sun, Jupiter, Saturn, and finally the stellatum, the sphere of the stars.

According to the Ptolemaic model, the orbit of the moon marked the boundary between the earthly and the celestial realms. Everything beyond the moon was eternal and immutable: everything below the moon's orbit was subject to change and decay. The spheres increased in rank and dimension the further away from the earth they were. This was a universe of clear boundaries between the realms and between the spheres. This was the universe known by the early Church, and, as a basic model, it lasted right through the Middle Ages.

An accusation often made against the old cosmology is that it was earth centered—and so it can appear from a glance at a map of the spheres. But in the medieval model, which developed from the scheme mapped out by Ptolemy, beyond the stellatum was the Primum Mobile, or First Movable, and beyond that was the realm of God where all earthly ideas about space and time broke down. All motion in the universe came from God and was transmitted by the Primum Mobile down through the spheres. The earth was the furthest sphere from the realm of God, which meant that it occupied the lowest place in the universe, in keeping with man's fallen status. Dante placed Satan at the center of the earth, the absolute lowest point. In the strictest sense, the earth was outside the heavens, at the bottom of the celestial pile. In the medieval universe, up and down really mattered. The longed-for destination of the soul was beyond. This was an aspirational universe.

The medieval cathedral was a microcosm of the medieval universe. Its elaborate west façade emphasized that the pilgrim was entering another realm, synonymous with the celestial realm that lay beyond the orbit of the moon. Symbolically the world lay in the west and was outside the door just as the earth was outside the heavens and occupied the lowest place in the universe. Once inside, the narthex or porch functioned as an intermediate place, to allow for adjustment and for earthly business to be conducted under Heaven's gaze. Then the pilgrim passed into the nave, the main body of the church, and then toward the sanctuary, which was shielded behind an elaborately carved and decorated rood screen, so profound were the mysteries enacted there. This, the most sacred place on earth, was the preserve of the clergy.

However one feature of the medieval church was the frequency and number of processions during which the clergy would leave their sanctuary and process through the main body of the church, then outside, and through the town or settlement, followed by the people in their guilds and groups or as individuals. In this way, the sanctuary and the world would be united and the belief emphasized that everyone is on a journey to God.

From the evidence of the early Church and the medieval periods, it cannot be deduced that until a certain moment somewhere around the middle of the twentieth century every church ever built was oriented along an east/west axis. Site restrictions in towns and cities had already begun to make this impossible, and the eastward orientation was adopted less frequently during the Baroque period. But throughout the centuries, the symbolism of priest and people facing the same direction remained.

The enthusiasm for the dismantling of the old universal model may partly have been due to a human desire to be elevated through the celestial ranks, even if this eventually resulted in a complete dismantling of the heavens. In *The Pearly Gates of Cyber Space*, Margaret Wertheim describes the development of Western universal space from the towering splendors of the medieval universe as described by Dante, to the boundless infinity of the contemporary model. In this process, she claims, Christian soul-space has been lost. In her account of the development of the Relativist universe she writes,

> By homogenising space and reducing "place" to a strict mathematical formalism, we have robbed our universe of *meaning* and taken away any sense of intrinsic directionality. The flip side of our cosmological democracy is thus an existential anarchy. With no place more special than any other, there is no place ultimately to aim for—no goal, no destination, no end. The cosmological principle that once rescued us from the gutter of the universe has left us, in the final instance, with *no place to go*.[5]

[5] Margaret Wertheim, *The Pearly Gates of Cyberspace: A History of Space from Dante to the Internet* (London: Virago Press, 1999), 185.

6

Reclaiming Sacred Space

According to James Hitchcock in *The Decline and Fall of Radical Catholicism,*

> religious renewal since the Council has been on one level a frank snobbery in which the well-educated, articulate, relatively young have unquestioningly assumed their own moral, religious, and human superiority over the silent majority. An elderly widow disturbed over the suppression of novena services in her parish is at best patronized, and is often told that she has no choice but to update her piety.... When progressives speak of the Church's insensitivity to human needs and its rigidity they mean exclusively its insensitivity to their own needs.... The masses in the Church are assumed to have emotional needs which are in principle invalid, and the reformer's prescription for them is simply conversion.[1]

This is a damming indictment if ever there was one, but an uncomfortably familiar one. Practically every revolutionary upheaval of the modern age has been led by members of the educated middle class claiming to act on behalf of "the people" against an established elite. And what is more, the promoters of revolution who really want power themselves, particularly despise those among "the

[1] James Hitchcock, *The Decline and Fall of Radical Catholicism* (New York: Image Books, Doubleday, 1972), 85.

people" who refuse to join the revolt, those who like things the way they are.

It is often said that the aristocracy and the working class have a lot in common. They both like highly decorated homes and churches; both tend to resist change unless it is absolutely necessary; and neither are fond of becoming involved in leisure time activities that prevent them from "hanging around" on their estates, whether country or inner-city. Instead it is the middle classes who prefer bare walls and plain furniture and shudder at any obvious sign of either elite or popular taste and piety. It is the middle classes who agitate for changes they are going to benefit from, and the middle classes who like getting involved.

James Hitchcock has also observed this:

> The "Catholic Revolution" has in reality been two-pronged, with the prongs pointed in opposite directions. It is the revolt of the elite middle against the authoritarian hierarchy above and the ignorant masses below. As such it follows a classic revolutionary pattern, including the fact that the revolt masquerades as a spontaneous popular uprising, while concealing the fact that special groups will be its beneficiaries.[2]

The "Graced by the Spirit Process" underway in Westminster Diocese aims to involve more lay people in the running of parishes. Once promoted as beneficial for its own sake and a sign of renewal in the Church, lay activity is now deemed a necessity because amid the talk of "awakening the gifts of lay people in a new and creative way" is the fact that parishes will have to merge and some will have to close because of a shortage of priests.

[2] Ibid., 90.

Yet priests already enjoy the services of pastoral assis-
tants, catechetic coordinators, liturgy coordinators, young
adults' coordinators, and others. And anecdotal evidence
suggests that some priests enjoy them less than others. One
parish priest who tried wearing a cassock was told, "We
don't want any of that around here, Father." Another who
objected to a mime being acted out by parish youth before
the final blessing at Mass was advised to update his ideas.
And at least one prospective candidate for the priesthood
was so put off by the prospect of dealing with an "active lay
apostolate" that he abandoned his vocation. Meanwhile, look
what has happened to the popular devotions and practices
that once nourished working-class Catholic life in particular. And lay people who try to bring back some of the
traditional practices are similarly ridiculed. For example, in
one parish a group of parents who wanted to dispense with
guitar-accompanied hymns and reintroduce Gregorian chant
for the benefit of the young were told to "liberate their
attitudes". In another parish where the reordering of the
church interior was being discussed, any mention of actually liking the interior as it was would be met by the accusation of being "attached to the appearances and having no
understanding of the importance of the essences".

The irony is that in recent decades, while a minority of
lay people have become actively involved in the various committees and groups that dominate parish life, many more
have drifted away, and vocations have plummeted. Meanwhile the prescription is more of the same, more active lay
involvement. There are no figures to show how many took
part in the "Graced by the Spirit" consultation, beyond the
fact that 74% of Westminster parishes responded. But in
one parish, where Sunday Mass attendance averages eight
hundred, eighty people attended the consultation meeting,

and this was deemed a great success. Yet this represents a response of only 10% of parishioners.

One aspect of the recent reforms that quickly becomes apparent is their emphasis on self-improvement. Expressions like "empowering the laity" and "unleashing the creativity of the People of God" are used again and again and could almost have come straight out of the many self-help manuals crowding the shelves of contemporary bookshops. Another feature is the emphasis on the spoken word in the new liturgy. Everything must be amplified and spelled out, even if that means turning up the volume on the sound system in an age when there are so few opportunities to find silence and contemplation.

The evolutionary and revolutionary view of history holds that since everything, including mankind, is evolving, today's point of view must be more advanced than yesterday's. This process requires an enlightened group of individuals to overthrow the old and established order at certain key moments in history, and during such periods of turmoil there are bound to be casualties. Therefore, if today's generation is more capable of discerning God's will for mankind than previous generations, it again has to follow that anyone who adheres to the beliefs and customs of the past and has not adopted the new way of thinking, must be ignorant, stubborn, or, as yet, insufficiently educated. These people must therefore catch on to the new (and therefore better) ways of doing things or be allowed to fall by the wayside.

But there lies something of a contradiction in the Modernist argument. For if human understanding is always evolving, then why advocate a return to the so-called untainted and simple forms of the very early Church as so many of the reformers do? Cardinal Ratzinger points this out in *The Spirit of the Liturgy*:

As I see it, the problem with a large part of modern
liturgiology is that it tends to recognize only antiquity as
a source, and therefore normative, and to regard everything developed later, in the Middle Ages and through
the Council of Trent, as decadent. And so one ends up
with dubious reconstructions of the most ancient practice, fluctuating criteria, and never-ending suggestions for
reform, which lead ultimately to the disintegration of
the liturgy that has evolved in a living way.[3]

It is part of the Modernist impulse in general to recognize the most distant past as an inspiration for the future
and to dismiss the intervening millennia as irrelevant. Church
reformers, obeying the same impulse, are faced with a problem, however. The secular Modernists essentially want to
dismiss Christian tradition, and this prompts them to look
back to a pre-Christian antiquity. But those who would
reform the Church have less scope for the kind of wish
fulfillment that comes from projecting contemporary, uto-
pian ideas onto a past that can only ever be known from
the fragments of stone that have survived it. Mass facing
the people really was not the practice of the early Church
as the reformers claim it was.

James Hitchcock again:

The open, tolerant, democratic spirit which was supposed to characterize Church renewal should have dictated a tactful abandonment of the old piety on the part
of the reformers, along with at minimum a silent accep-
tance of it as a possible valid way for other men. Instead
liturgists who gained power often tried to suppress the
old devotions totally and systematically, while those out

[3] Joseph Cardinal Ratzinger, *The Spirit of the Liturgy* (San Francisco: Ignatius Press, 2000), 82.

of power waged a running propaganda battle against them.... Liturgical change was also carried out rather dishonestly by many reformers. Originally, they told conservatives that popular devotions were invalid because they were theologically unsound historical accretions, dating from the late Middle Ages, the Baroque era, or the Romantic nineteenth century, while the aim of liturgical change was to return as far as possible to the authentic worship of the early Church. Only gradually did many liturgists reveal that their true aim was to construct a liturgy in as thoroughly modern an idiom as possible and that they cared little about the liturgies of the early Church.[4]

Pope Leo XIII, Pope Pius X, and Pope Pius XII each spoke out against Modernism. And during the postconciliar period, attempts have been made to reign in some of the more obvious abuses that have accompanied the changes. In 1997, for example, Pope John Paul II promulgated the *Instruction on Certain Questions Regarding the Collaboration of the Non-Ordained Faithful in the Sacred Ministry of Priests*. The *Instruction* stresses the distinction between the ordained priesthood and the common priesthood of the people[5] and requires that this distinction should not be blurred in practice. For instance, lay people may not give the homily at Mass, and extraordinary ministers of Holy Communion are to be just that, "extraordinary". According to the *Instruction*,

extraordinary ministers may distribute Holy Communion at Eucharistic celebrations only when there are no

[4] Hitchcock, *Decline and Fall*, 92.

[5] Pope John Paul II, "Theological Principles", in *Instruction on Certain Questions Regarding the Collaboration of the Non-Ordained Faithful in the Sacred Ministry of Priests* (Boston: Pauline Books and Media, 1997).

ordained ministers present or when those ordained ministers present at a liturgical celebration are truly unable to distribute Holy Communion. They may also exercise this function at Eucharistic celebrations where there are particularly large numbers of the faithful and which would be excessively prolonged because of an insufficient number of ordained ministers to distribute Holy Communion.[6]

The same paragraph also states, "To avoid creating confusion, certain practices are to be avoided and eliminated where such have emerged in particular Churches:—extraordinary ministers receiving Holy Communion apart from the other faithful as though concelebrants;—the habitual use of extraordinary ministers of Holy Communion. . . ." However, this appears to have had little effect in the parishes where the practice of "the habitual use of extraordinary ministers of Holy Communion" is still widespread.

Also of concern to the Vatican are the translations into vernacular of liturgical texts carried out immediately after the Council. According to *Liturgiam Authenticam*, which was published by the Congregation for Divine Worship and the Discipline of the Sacraments in 2001, the main areas of concern are the faithfulness of the texts to the original Latin, their loss of theological content and meaning, and the suitability of their use of everyday and currently fashionable language.[7]

Eamon Duffy, reader in Church history at the University of Cambridge and a fellow of Magdalene College, welcomes the use of the vernacular in the liturgy. However in

[6] Ibid., "Practical Provisions", art. 8, par. 2.
[7] Congregation for Divine Worship and the Discipline of the Sacraments, *Liturgiam Authenticam: On the Use of Vernacular Languages in the Publication of the Books of the Roman Liturgy* (London: Catholic Truth Society, 2001).

his essay "Rewriting the Liturgy: The Theological Implications of Translation", he writes:

> it seems to me that the actual moment at which the
> transition to the vernacular occurred could hardly have
> been less propitious. The post-conciliar transformation
> of Catholic liturgy, theology and ecclesiology coincided
> with a period of profound cultural dislocation in the
> West. Genuine theological renewal became inextricably
> entangled with a shallow and philistine repudiation of
> the past which was to have consequences as disastrous
> in theology as they were in the fine arts, architecture
> and city planning. Thus the sub-Christian aridities of
> neo-scholastic seminary textbooks were exchanged for
> a mess of paperbacks, and pious psychobabble replaced
> the smug certainties of the older orthodoxy. There was
> a widespread and undiscriminating collapse of confi-
> dence in Catholic theological tradition, and, as a result,
> some of the least happy developments within the
> Churches of the Reformation, and indeed within the
> secular culture of the 1960s and early 1970s, were eagerly
> embraced as theologically progressive—signs of the times,
> stirrings of the spirit.[8]

"Rewriting the Liturgy" includes a number of examples
of prayers from the 1973 Missal that have been translated
into English in a way that emphasizes the "primacy of human
religious activity or experience, at the expense of the Latin
Missal's relentless emphasis on the agency of God."[9] To
give just one example here, the Collect for the Eleventh
Sunday in Ordinary Time appears in Latin as:

---

[8] Eamon Duffy, "Rewriting the Liturgy: The Theological Implications of
Translation", in *Beyond the Prosaic*, ed. Stratford Caldecott (Edinburgh: T and T
Clark, 1998), 100.

[9] Ibid., 107.

> Deus in te sperantium fortitude, invocationibus
>   nostris adesto propitius,
> et, quia sine te nihil potest mortalis infirmitas,
> gratiae tua praesta semper auxilium,
> ut, in exsequendis mandatis tuis,
> et voluntate tibi et actione placeamus.

The essay then offers the following translation,

O God, the strength of all them that put their trust in thee,
mercifully accept our prayers,
and because through the weakness of our mortal nature
we can do no good thing without thee,
grant us the help of thy grace,
that in keeping of thy commandments we may please thee,
both in will and deed;
Through Jesus Christ our Lord.

This is followed by the version in the 1973 Missal,

Almighty God, our hope and our strength,
without you we falter.
Help us to follow Christ and to live according to your will.

Eamon Duffy then comments:

The inadequacy and inaccuracy of this translation almost
beggars belief, but there is more here than ineptitude.
At every point in the prayer the insistence of the original on the impotence for good of unaided human nature,
and on the primacy of grace, is weakened or downright
contradicted. God is not now "the strength of them that
put their trust in thee", but, much more vaguely, "our
hope and our strength": strength is not seen here as
proceeding from hope, but as a parallel quality. The
stern insistence of the original that without God "mortal
frailty can do *nothing*"—"nihil potest mortalis infirmitas"

becomes the feeble "without you we falter". Grace is no longer even mentioned, the strong phrase "auxilium gratiae" becoming a simple "help us", while the reference to the following of the commandments is edited out, being replaced by a phrase about "following Christ" which has no warrant in the original. The insistence of the original that the external following of the commandments, under grace, can become not merely an external obedience, but a means of pleasing God "both in will and in deed" is thus totally lost, the pairing of our actions and will becoming blurred into an unfocussed reference to the will of God. In short, a magnificently balanced Augustinian meditation on the dialectic of grace and obedience becomes a vague and semi-Pelagian petition for help in case we falter.[10]

The question must surely be whether something more fundamental than the spirit of the times, that is, of the 1960s and 1970s, was at work or whether it was the spirit of the age that found its most full expression during that period. Whatever the answer, there cannot be much doubt that the new liturgy and the new theology informing it represent a definite departure from tradition. The differences can be summed up as the following;

— according to tradition, mankind is fallen, whereas the new view is that mankind, if not already partly divine, is at least privy to the divine realm by virtue of possessing a desire for that realm;

— tradition holds that of itself human nature can achieve no good, whereas the new idea is that the relationship between Man and God involves some kind of

[10] Ibid., 110–11.

partnership in which Man's intentions and effort are brought to fruition with God's help;

— according to tradition, Man is a pilgrim in the world who must recognize the wonders of God's creation but at the same time be fully aware that Heaven, not this world, is his end. The new idea, instead, is that mankind and God can work together to make the world a better place and achieve a version of Heaven here on earth.

The question also concerns Man's place in the universe as well as his relation to God. If the main impulse behind the new theology is of the self-promotion of mankind, this cannot be divorced from the contemporary idea of a universe that has been emptied of the divine. In a universe in which sacred space cannot exist, in a universe that has been desacralized, the only sacred realm possible is within the individual. Inevitably then, the new liturgy and the new church building must also be desacralized to reflect this. Desacralization is therefore the inevitable consequence of Relativism, as is a turning away from the emptied and meaningless universe beyond the earth.

"Are we not interested in the cosmos any more?" asks Cardinal Ratzinger in *The Spirit of the Liturgy*. "Are we today really hopelessly huddled in our own little circle? Is it not important, precisely today, to pray with the whole of creation? Is it not important, precisely today, to find room for the dimension of the future, for hope in the Lord who is to come again, to recognize again, indeed to live, the dynamism of the new creation as an essential form of the liturgy?" [11]

---

[11] Ratzinger, *Spirit of the Liturgy*, 82.

In "The Catholicity of the Liturgy: Shaping a New Agenda", M. Francis Mannion observes:

> One of the most remarkable features of the pre-conciliar liturgical movement was the resurgence of interest in the eschatological character of Christian worship, generated in great part by a new appreciation of the liturgical life of the East. Yet that interest seemed to be diverted soon after the Second Vatican Council as eschatology began to be secularised and politicised, and as Catholic life and worship generally began to refocus in the direction of relevance to modern culture.
>
> Related to the eschatological is the renewal of the cosmic sense in the liturgy. Catholic liturgy today notably suffers from a shrunken cosmic consciousness and a shrunken cosmic ritualisation. A more adequate cosmic expressivity will serve to draw all of creation, including the saintly and angelic, into the framework of worship. A renewed cosmic emphasis will help overcome the present tendency of liturgical celebration toward privatisation and congregationalist self-referentiality and self-enclosure.[12]

This lack of cosmic awareness is also a reflection of what the astronomers of today never tire of saying, that our planet orbits an insignificant sun in an average-sized galaxy that is nowhere in particular in a universe that extends forever in every direction. No wonder the overwhelming tendency is to acknowledge that there is a lot of space out there, shrug the shoulders, and turn away.

Fantastically powerful telescopes that could pick out a cricket ball on the other side of the world gather streams of

---

[12] M. Francis Mannion, "The Catholicity of the Liturgy: Shaping a New Agenda", in *Beyond the Prosaic*, 29.

data from space. We are told that our own galaxy is 100,000 light-years across and that the most distant observable galaxy is 18,000,000,000 light-years away, which makes a lot of zeros, given that a light-year, being the distance that light travels in a year, is 9,000,000,000,000 kilometers (nearly 6,000,000,000,000 miles). We are also told that there are 100,000,000,000 stars in our galaxy alone and 1,000,000,000 galaxies in the observable universe. But again these numbers are as impossible to comprehend as the quantities they convey.

Not only is there nothing much out there but more and forever more of the same, but also our planet has been so blanketed by the glare of artificial light that if you live in a town or a city, or close to one, you will not see more than a handful of the stars visible to the naked eye. The wonders of the night sky, the greatest show not on earth, which our ancestors took for granted, have become only memories. The universe has grown dark and silent; it may be the most measured and quantified universe in history, but it is surely the least known.

Today the cosmic realm exists only in science fiction and the cinema. Writers and directors trawl the ancient mythologies for storylines to set in space, which becomes the backdrop for the hero's journey, a realm where good battles against evil and where monsters and dragons lurk. Since the Galileo affair, the Church has all but abandoned space to the scientists, who have succeeded in emptying the universe of all meaning with the consequence that the human imagination, uneasy with the resulting void, has filled it again. God may have been evicted from the cosmic realm, but Man has invented all manner of extraterrestrial beings to replace Him.

In *The Discarded Image*, C. S. Lewis discusses the changing model of the universe:

We are all, very properly, familiar with the idea that in every age the human mind is deeply influenced by the accepted Model of the universe. But there is a two-way traffic; the Model is also affected by the prevailing temper of mind. We must recognise that what has been called "a taste in universes" is not only pardonable but inevitable. We can no longer dismiss the change of Models as a simple progress from error to truth. No Model is a catalogue of ultimate realities, and none is a mere fantasy. Each is a serious attempt to get in all the phenomena known at a given period and each succeeds in getting in a great many. But also, no less surely, each reflects the prevalent psychology of an age almost as much as it reflects the state of that age's knowledge.[13]

Lewis goes on to speculate on the passing of the current model, which, he predicts, will come about when the inner need for a new one becomes sufficiently great. Then the evidence to support a new model will turn up, not by magic, but because the questions being asked will be different and the answers being sought will be found in hitherto-unknown places.

The fact that a couple of scientists have already suggested that the speed of light may not always be constant, that at around the time of the Big Bang the speed of light may have varied, and that this could have implications for the authority of Einstein's theories of relativity, may not be greatly significant according to Lewis' argument. All that really needs to be agreed upon is that the Relativist universe no longer suits us.

[13] C. S. Lewis, *The Discarded Image: An Introduction to Medieval and Renaissance Literature* (Cambridge: Canto, imprint of Cambridge University Press, 1994), 222.

The time for that is surely now, or could be if we wished. The current model does not even have to change because, ironically, all points of view have equal value in a Relativist universe, and it must be entirely permissible to live in a sacred universe if we choose. Therefore it is already an entirely valid point of view to hold that the universe is filled with angels and saints and that the planets and galaxies are moved, not merely by the force of gravity, but also by the love of God.

To resacralize the liturgy and the church building, two things are required. The first is a leap of the imagination into universal space in order to insist that it be resacralized, that it be recognized as the sacred realm it never stopped being. Because in order to reclaim sacred space within the church building, cosmic sacred space must also be reclaimed. And in order to resacralize the liturgy, the cosmic liturgy must also be heard again.

The second is to put aside the desire for self-promotion that the new theology embodies and both the new liturgy and the new church building express. Combined together, these two requirements involve the simultaneous acts of thinking bigger and being smaller, thinking big enough to embrace the cosmos and being small enough to fit into it. At present the situation is the reverse: everyone is thinking small and acting big. And just look at the results.

*   *   *

The modern mind may not be made up on the subject of the Relativist universe, but it knows where it stands on the architecture of Relativist space. It was over the issue of space that the Modernist style finally fell. The aesthetics of the style had been the subject of bitter criticism for years. But it was the realization that Modernist ideas about space produce dysfunctional environments that brought about its end.

Jane Jacobs first coined the term "defensible space" in the 1970s.[14] Her claim was that the abandonment of traditional urban forms and the adoption of Modernist principles of free-flowing space had left people adrift in endless and unbounded seas of concrete without the ability to influence or control the environment around them. In no time at all, entire neighborhoods and urban centers redeveloped by the architects and planners of the 1950s and '60s had become virtual wastelands as their inhabitants reacted with loathing against the Modernist vision imposed on them.

Architects like Le Corbusier, Mies van der Rohe, and Walter Gropius had advocated sweeping away the traditional urban patterns of streets, squares, avenues, courtyards, et cetera, and replacing them with primary, geometric forms located in space as functional requirements dictated. The result was supposed to "liberate space" and the inhabitants, who would be able to breathe the fresher, newer air of the unbounded, nonhierarchical, egalitarian city.

The result was lots of concrete blocks of flats surrounded by empty acres of grass and/or concrete belonging to no one and consequently open to everyone and everything. The problem, as Jane Jacobs pointed out, was that the shiny, new dwellings, functional as they were, provided no "defensible space" for the inhabitants. The old street patterns and tenement buildings had been able to differentiate between public space, semi–public space, and private space. A street

---

[14] Jane Jacobs, *The Life and Death of Great American Cities* (New York: Random House, 1961).

could "belong" to the residents in a way that the acres of unbounded space on the new estates could not. And yet at the same time it remained a public space. A tenement court-yard is a communal area, and yet residents have a level of control over who enters it and what goes on there.

To create "defensible space" and give people a stake in their neighborhoods, it was therefore essential to distin-guish between the private, semi-private, and public and to create boundaries between them. "We must re-create a hier-archy of spaces", architects began to say more and more as the 1970s became the 1980s. And the only way to do this was by rediscovering traditional urban forms and creating streets and squares and avenues and courtyards again.

In the secular world, many of the worst examples of Mod-ernist design have already been demolished, and more demo-litions are scheduled. One of the first to go, and the cause of much debate at the time, was the Pruitt-Igoe housing development in Saint Louis, Missouri, which was built in 1955 and designed by Minoru Yamasaki, the architect of the World Trade Center. The 14-story steel, concrete, and glass blocks separated by open spaces of green lawn were so hated by the people who lived in them that when the Saint Louis authorities finally asked them what they wanted, they replied "demolish them". And that is what happened. In 1973, the authorities blew them up.

The demolition of the Pruitt-Igoe housing development was a turning point, and now there is nothing unusual about the demise of yet another visionary urban development of the 1960s or 1970s. One commentator at the time claimed that modern architecture had caused more damage to Lon-don than the Luftwaffe.

Something similar could be said about the effect of Mod-ernism on churches. "We must recreate a hierarchy of spaces."

If only church architects would come to their senses the way the secular architects did over twenty years ago. But churchgoers do not vandalize or set fire to their Modernist buildings. Instead they walk away from them.

A church building is not a temple in the pagan sense of being the dwelling place of the deity where only the priesthood may venture. Neither is a church building exclusively a meeting house for the people to gather. By focusing on the idea of a "gathering place for the People of God", contemporary liturgists have largely obliterated the fact that the Mass is, first and foremost, a sacrifice. There can be no sacrificial meal without the offering of the victim. To deny this is to render the meal meaningless beyond the level of a communal gathering.

The blurring of the distinction between the nave and sanctuary in modern churches essentially represents a blurring of the distinction between the priesthood and the people, which in turn represents a denial of the Mass as a sacrifice. Universal liturgical space in which all boundaries are dissolved, implies a universal priesthood. But the priest by virtue of his ordination offers a sacrifice that is entirely distinct from that offered by the people, who offer themselves. To reclaim the fact that the Mass is a sacrifice, the priesthood has to be set apart again as having a unique function not shared by the laity. To do this, it is necessary to reclaim the sanctuary as sacred space, designated as sacred by being set apart from the nave and rendered sacred by the sacrifice enacted there.

"We must recreate a hierarchy of spaces", the secular architects said twenty years ago in a different context. But the same principle applies here. Free-flowing, universal space is the same everywhere, and, at the same time, nothing in particular anywhere. Similarly, if every part of the church building is equally sacred, then no part of it can be truly sacred. The ghastliness of so much contemporary church architecture is a reflection of the vision that informs it, a vision that is earth-bound and Man-centered. It therefore cannot even *hope* to speak to the modern age, or any other age, because it is so dreary. There is no other way of saying it. But there is a solution, and it is a simple one. If today's churches deny the transcendent vision, which they do, then the task is to reclaim that vision. Similarly, if the design of churches today has brought about a dissolution of sacred space, which it has, then the task is to reclaim that as well.

In some parishes in the United States the first steps toward achieving this have been taken as churches reordered in the 1970s are restored to their original forms. Reordered church interiors are being remodeled to re-create a hierarchy of spaces; distinctions between altar and nave are being redrawn by replacing altar rails and relocating tabernacles to their rightful place; and the message that the church is a sacred building is being spoken again as ceiling panels erected to hide ornate vaulted ceilings are ripped out, whitewash is cleaned away to reveal frescos and wall paintings, and statues and elaborate high altars are reintroduced.

This is not to say that for the design of new churches architects should merely copy the styles of the past and design according to, say, the Gothic style or the Romanesque, although this might not be a bad idea in the meantime. It took the secular architects at least a couple of decades to develop a contemporary style that combined tried and tested spatial principles with contemporary aesthetics, and even today there is no single style that could be described as "modern" (as opposed to Modernist). The essential thing is to get the spaces right, and, in time, the aesthetics will follow. As for those Modernist church buildings that cannot be adapted for use in a sacred universe, a universe that has been derelativized, ... well, many Modernist architects in the secular sphere have lived to see their creations demolished too.

1
Demolition of the Pruitt-Igoe housing development, Saint Louis, Missouri, U.S.A., 1972.

7

Turn Again, Father

Exclusivity has taken on a particular form in the postconciliar Church. In seeking to dismantle the traditional hierarchies and dissolve the boundaries between the priesthood and the laity, between the Church and the world, and between the Church and other religions, the reformers have pursued the supposedly egalitarian model of the group as the preferred organizational structure. There are prayer groups, outreach groups, peace and justice groups, women's groups, liturgy groups, youth groups, spirituality groups— all kinds of groups. And there are experts who address the various groups, and committees who discuss the recommendations of the groups. And when these groups meet, more often than not they will sit in a circle, because circles are supposed to be nonhierarchical. They are also the favored form of therapy and encounter groups.

The circular form has its own dynamic, which is all toward the center. While this suits the inwardness of so much modern spirituality, the trouble is that once the center is reached, one can go no further. The only direction forward leads back to the circumference. Movement within the circular form is either constantly to and from the center, or round and round, and both ultimately lead nowhere. And yet circles are difficult to break out of, since the form inevitably turns its back on the beyond.

Circles are the most exclusive forms going. Firstly, everyone in a group circle necessarily sits with his back to the outside. Secondly, there's no point in belonging to a group circle unless you share its aims, and the tendency is to assume that those on the outside are opposed to these aims. Thirdly, joining the group circle is no simple matter, because a circle can only be enlarged if it is first broken and then reformed. This gives existing members the power to vet and obstruct new entrants. Linear forms, on the other hand, can accept additions endlessly without disrupting the original form, and as a result they are more accommodating to the newcomer, who can join or fall away at will. Linear hierarchies also have the advantage of being visible. When power is in the hands of groups unconnected by any discernible structure, it is hard to know what influence they have and over what they wield it.

Attend Mass at an unfamiliar parish church, and all too often the impression is of nonstop activity by a small number of parishioners, while everyone else remains as passive as the entire laity was supposed to have been before the changes. It is not entirely unknown for a powerful group of lay people in a parish to set the agenda for everyone else, or for priests who have tried to foster tradition in parishes to have been transferred elsewhere as the result of complaints to the local bishop from such groups.

The emptied church buildings of the age, with their meaningless spaces and their refusal to connect with what is beyond, encourage so much activity. Blanket lighting and sound systems reach into every corner, mirroring the world outside, which is lit up twenty-four hours a day and filled with noise. The resulting sensory overload either generates more activity or results in burnout. Many churches built in the 1960s and 1970s already look dated, and if they were secular buildings they would have been demolished or radically reworked by now. And the newest churches still embody Relativist space that is homogenous, directionless, and value-free. Whatever engineering feats they demonstrate or ingenious forms their vast expanses of plain walling and clear glass create, they cannot achieve what the most ordinary traditional church building managed—the creation of sacred space here on earth that at the same time points to a sacred and divine realm beyond the earth. They cannot do this because the principles informing their design deny that sacred space exists, either here or elsewhere.

The reclamation of the transcendent vision cannot be achieved without a reorientation toward the transcendent, and this requires the ending of the disastrous and entirely novel practice of Mass facing the people and returning to the traditional liturgical direction in which priest and people together face the east. It means a re-turning of priest and people to God. Thankfully a rising generation of young scholars is now studying the traditions of the Church and beginning to shoot holes in many of the modernizers' arguments. For instance, U. M. Lang, a priest at the London Oratory where the sanctuary remains intact and the New Mass is celebrated *versus orientem*, has recently published *Turning towards the Lord: Orientation in Liturgical Prayer*. In this highly researched work he makes the point that while the symbolism of praying to the east had begun to be lost by the Baroque period, particularly in urban sites where churches could not always be constructed along an east/west axis, the symbolism of the common direction of prayer was recognized and retained. He also discusses the theology of the practice:

> Each Eucharist is offered for the praise and glory of God's name, for the benefit of us and of the holy Church as a whole.... Theologically, the Mass as a whole, the Liturgy of the Word and the Liturgy of the Eucharist, is directed at the same time towards God and towards the

people. In the form of the celebration one must avoid a confusion of theology and topography, especially when the priest stands at the altar. The priest speaks to the people only during the dialogues at the altar. Everything else is prayer to the Father through Christ in the Holy Spirit. Evidently, it is most desirable that this theology should be expressed in the visible shape of the liturgy.

... When we speak to someone, we obviously face that person. Accordingly, the whole liturgical assembly, priest and people, should face the same way, turning towards God to whom prayers and offerings are addressed in this common act of trinitarian worship. [Cardinal] Ratzinger rightly protests against the mistaken idea that in this case the celebrating priest is facing "towards the altar", "towards the tabernacle", or even "towards the wall". The catchphrase often heard nowadays that the priest is "turning his back on the people" is a classic example of confounding theology and topography, for the crucial point is that the Mass is a common act of worship where priest and people together, representing the pilgrim Church, reach out for the transcendent God.[1]

U. M. Lang's conclusion is that the readoption of the common direction of liturgical prayer is highly desirable, if not crucial to the well-being of the Church.

There is a widespread consensus that the dialogue parts between priest and people and the proclamation of the Word of God require a face-to-face position. So the Introductory Rites and the Liturgy of the Word should best be conducted from the sedilia and the ambo, as is now the case. It should also be taken for granted that for parts of the Communion Rite and for the Concluding Rite

[1] U. M. Lang, *Turning towards the Lord: Orientation in Liturgical Prayer* (San Francisco: Ignatius Press, 2004), 31–32.

the priest faces the people, according to the rubrics of the renewed *Missale Romanum*. However, for the Liturgy of the Eucharist in the strict sense, in particular the canon, it is more than fitting that the whole congregation, including the celebrant, be directed towards the Lord, and that is expressed by turning towards the altar—whether it is actually oriented or only indicates the "liturgical" east. Hence the celebrant should not face the people during this part of the Mass....

This suggested combination of priest and people facing each other during the Liturgy of the Word and turning jointly towards the altar during the Liturgy of the Eucharist is not only a legitimate option in the *Novus Ordo Missae* of Pope Paul VI; it has also been approved explicitly by the Roman Congregation for Divine Worship.[2]

By their fruits shall you know them. The fruits of Relativist space and its embodiment in the contemporary church building have surely been the ugliest and emptiest churches in history. In order to begin alleviating this building disaster, which has given us churches barely worthy of the name, one crucial first step has to be taken.

Turn again, Father.

[2] Ibid., 122–23.

1
Illustration of traditional priestly orientation.

ACKNOWLEDGMENTS

I would like to thank the following individuals for their help and support during the preparation of *No Place for God*: Earnest and Mary Carey, Anthony Delarue, Canon John MacDonald, the late Alice Thomas Ellis, Father Michael Lang, the late Michael Davies, Celia Haddon, and Dr. Raymond Edwards.

The author and the publisher express their appreciation to the following for permission to reprint excerpts from the following works:

Catholic Truth Society, London, for *General Instruction of the Roman Missal*, trans. Clifford Howell, S.J. (1973), and *The Parish Church: Principles of Liturgical Design and Re-ordering* (1984).

Costello Publishing Co., Inc., Northpoint, N.Y., for *Vatican Council: The Conciliar and Post Conciliar Documents*, edited by Austin Flannery, O.P. (1992).

Breda Ennis, professor of fine arts at the American University of Rome, for "A Vacuum in the Spirit: The Design of the Jubilee Church in Rome", *Sacred Architecture*, no. 9 (2004), as well as for several photos.

[Farrar, Straus and Giroux, LLC, New York, and] The Random House Group Ltd., Rushden, for *From Bauhaus to*

Our House by Tom Wolfe (1983); first published in U.K. by Jonathan Cape (1982).

Golgonooza Press, Ipswich, U.K., for *Chartres and the Birth of the Cathedral* by Titus Burckhardt (1995).

Gracewing Publishing, Leominster, England, for *Catholic Thought Since the Enlightenment: A Survey* by Aidan Nichols, O.P. (1998).

Professor Susan Henderson, for "Architecture and Theosophy: An Introduction", *Architronic Magazine* 8, no. 1 (January 1999), http://architronic.saed.kent.edu/.

James Hitchcock, for *The Decline and Fall of Radical Catholicism* (New York: Image Books, Doubleday, 1972).

Joseph Rykwert, for "The Dark Side of the Bauhaus", in *The Necessity of Artifice: Ideas in Architecture* (London: Academy Editions, 1982).

Sophia Institute Press, Manchester, N.H., for *Ugly As Sin: Why They Changed Our Churches from Sacred Places to Meeting Spaces—and How We Can Change Them Back Again* by Michael Rose (copyright 2001 Michael S. Rose).

Tan Books, Rockford, Ill., for *The Catholic Sanctuary and the Second Vatican Council* by Michael Davies (1997).

Virago Press of the Time Warner Book Group UK (London) and W. W. Norton, for *The Pearly Gates of Cyberspace from Dante to the Internet* by Margaret Wertheim (1999).

Full publication details are given where these works are cited.

LIST OF ILLUSTRATIONS

Chapter One

1. Parish Church of Oberkirch, Basel, Switzerland.
   Interior before 1973 reordering.
   Reproduced by permission of Fr. Gaudron.

2. Parish Church of Oberkirch, Basel, Switzerland.
   Interior after 1973 reordering.
   Reproduced by permission of Fr. Gaudron.

3. Saint Joseph's Church, Epsom, Surrey, England, 2001.
   Exterior.
   Picture courtesy of W. S. Atkins, Architect.

4. Saint Joseph's Church, Epsom, Surrey, England, 2001.
   Interior.
   Picture courtesy of W. S. Atkins, Architect.

5. Saint John's Abbey, Collegeville, Minnesota, U.S.A.,
   1961.
   Architect—Marcel Breuer.
   Exterior.
   Reproduced by permission of Saint John's Abbey,
   Collegeville, Minnesota.

6. Saint John's Abbey, Collegeville, Minnesota, U.S.A., 1961.
   Architect—Marcel Breuer.
   Interior.
   Reproduced by permission of Saint John's Abbey, Collegeville, Minnesota.

7. Parish Church, Riola di Vergato, near Bologna, Italy, 1978.
   Architect—Alvar Aalto.
   Exterior.
   © Richard Bryant/Arcaid.

8. Parish Church, Riola di Vergato, near Bologna, Italy, 1978.
   Architect—Alvar Aalto.
   Interior.
   © Richard Einzig/Arcaid.

Chapter Three

1. Bauhaus school of design, Dessau, 1925–26.
   Architect—Walter Gropius.
   Picture courtesy of Mewes and www.wikipedia.com.

2. Postcard of the Weissenhof Estate, Stuttgart, 1927.
   Picture courtesy of www.wikipedia.com.

3. National Congress, Brasilia, Brazil, 1956–60.
   Architect—Oscar Niemeyer.
   Picture courtesy of Xenia Antunes and www.wikipedia.com.

Chapter Four

8. Basilica of Our Lady of Guadalupe, Mexico City, 1976.
   Architect—Pedro Ramírez Vásquez.
   Exterior.
   © Richard Wareham/Sylvia Cordaiy Photo Library.

9. Basilica of Our Lady of Guadalupe, Mexico City, 1976.
   Architect—Pedro Ramírez Vásquez.
   Interior.
   © Richard Wareham/Sylvia Cordaiy Photo Library.

10. Our Lady of the Angels Cathedral, Los Angeles, 2002.
    Architect—Raphael Moneo.
    Exterior.
    © John Edward Linden/Arcaid.

11. Our Lady of the Angels Cathedral, Los Angeles, 2002.
    Architect—Raphael Moneo.
    Interior.
    © John Edward Linden/Arcaid.

12. Padre Pio Pilgrimage Church, Puglia, Italy, 2004.
    Architects—The Renzo Piano Building Workshop.
    Photograph courtesy of www.wikipedia.com.

13. Chapel of Reconciliation, Walsingham, England, 1981.
    Exterior.
    Reproduced by permission from Roman Catholic
    National Shrine, Walsingham.

INDEX

Photographs are indicated in italic page references. Footnotes are shown with an "n" beside the page reference.